WHALES *and* DOLPHINS

A GUIDE TO THE BIOLOGY AND BEHAVIOUR OF CETACEANS

SWAN·HILL
PRESS

Texts and drawings
Maurizio Würtz and Nadia Repetto

Editors
Valeria Manferto De Fabianis
Laura Accomazzo

Graphic design
Anna Galliani
Clara Zanotti

Translation
Studio Traduzioni Vecchia, Milan

WHALES *and* DOLPHINS

CONTENTS

A

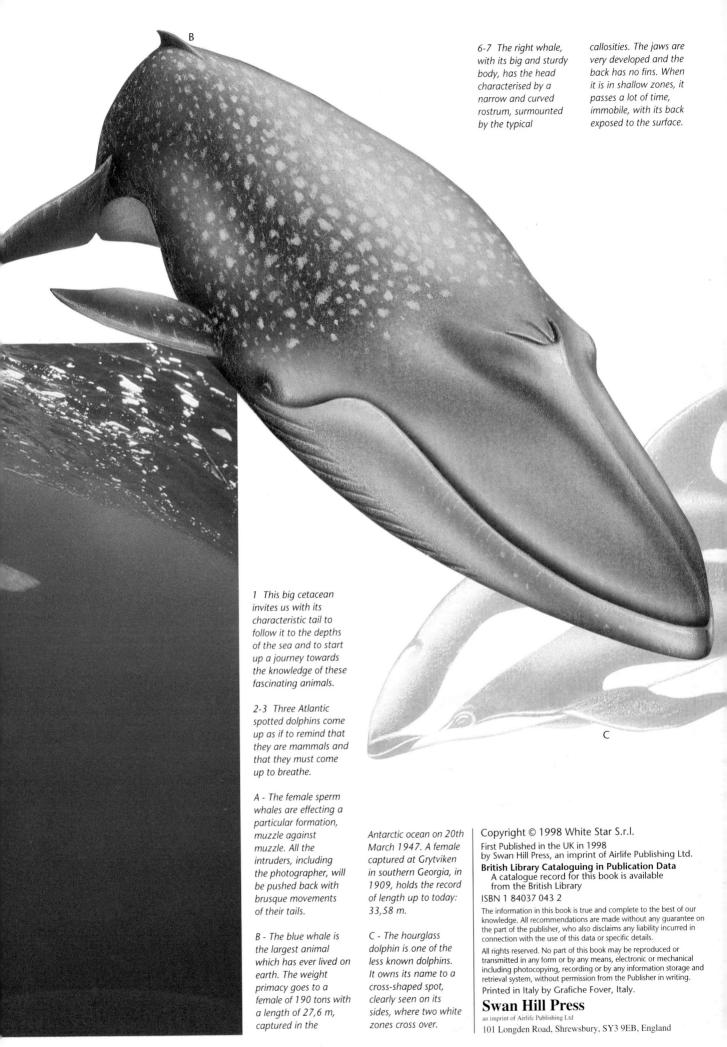

B

6-7 The right whale, with its big and sturdy body, has the head characterised by a narrow and curved rostrum, surmounted by the typical callosities. The jaws are very developed and the back has no fins. When it is in shallow zones, it passes a lot of time, immobile, with its back exposed to the surface.

1 This big cetacean invites us with its characteristic tail to follow it to the depths of the sea and to start up a journey towards the knowledge of these fascinating animals.

2-3 Three Atlantic spotted dolphins come up as if to remind that they are mammals and that they must come up to breathe.

A - The female sperm whales are effecting a particular formation, muzzle against muzzle. All the intruders, including the photographer, will be pushed back with brusque movements of their tails.

B - The blue whale is the largest animal which has ever lived on earth. The weight primacy goes to a female of 190 tons with a length of 27,6 m, captured in the Antarctic ocean on 20th March 1947. A female captured at Grytviken in southern Georgia, in 1909, holds the record of length up to today: 33,58 m.

C - The hourglass dolphin is one of the less known dolphins. It owns its name to a cross-shaped spot, clearly seen on its sides, where two white zones cross over.

C

Copyright © 1998 White Star S.r.l.
First Published in the UK in 1998 by Swan Hill Press, an imprint of Airlife Publishing Ltd.
British Library Cataloguing in Publication Data
A catalogue record for this book is available from the British Library
ISBN 1 84037 043 2

Printed in Italy by Grafiche Fover, Italy.

Swan Hill Press
an imprint of Airlife Publishing Ltd
101 Longden Road, Shrewsbury, SY3 9EB, England

FROM MYTH TO REALITY

There once was a young Greek musician named Arion, who lived on the island of Lesbos and played and sang like no other. It is said that after living in Corinth for some time as a guest at the court of King Periander, he decided to go to the colonies of Magna Grecia. In Sicily he won every contest against the greatest singers and musicians and received prizes and riches. Desirous to return to Greece, at Taraentum he embarked on a Corinthian ship with all his possessions. Unfortunately for him, the ship's crew were all pirates who decided to kill him and steal his possessions. Arion pleaded with them to take his riches but spare his life. They refused, but gave him the alternative of throwing himself into the sea. The musician then took up his lyre and played and sang so majestic a song that the crew was left speechless. He then leaped into the sea. A dolphin immediately allowed him to climb on its back and carried him safe and sound back to land, near Cape Matapan. From there he travelled back to Periander's court and told him of his adventures. When the pirates returned to Corinth, the king asked them for news of Arion. They said they had left him at Taraentum, but when the singer himself appeared before them, they had to admit the truth. Thus Arion regained his prizes and riches, thanks to the aid of a dolphin.

The legend of Arion, certainly the best known tale of its kind, most fully expresses the age-old bond between humans and dolphins. These animals were sacred to the Greeks, and their name is associated with the cult of Apollo in the city of Delphi near Mount Parnassus. We Westerners are most familiar with what Greek and Roman literature has bequeathed to us, but in reality dolphins are the protagonists of similar myths and legends from many coastal peoples all over the world, some of them dating back to 4000 years ago.

In addition to singers, dolphins have also inspired painters and sculptors. Cretan, Roman, Chinese and Indian art of the 4th and 5th centuries BC have left us realistic statues, paintings and mosaics of these animals. The custom of stamping the profile of a dolphin on coins as a token of good luck predates Greek culture and has survived up to this day.

B

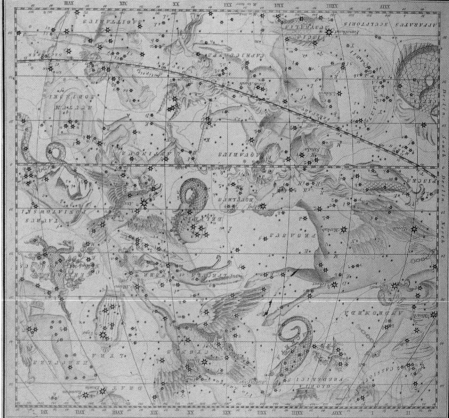

A

A - In ancient times, dolphins were often likened to female deities. In this mosaic from El Djem, Tunisia, the animal is associated with a Nereid, a sea nymph and daughter of Nereus and Doris.

B, F - The first to use a dolphin's aid was Poseidon, Neptune to the ancient Romans. When the sea god fell in love with the splendid black eyes of Amphitrite and decided to make her his wife, a dolphin found her and hid her in an underwater cave. Poseidon gave the dolphin the highest of honours: a place in the heavens as a constellation. In the northern hemisphere, the constellation Delphinus can be seen in July, between the Eagle and Pegasus.

C - In the 16th century, whales and dolphins were considered sea monsters, and thus did Albrecht Dürer (1471-1528), a famous German painter and engraver, interpret the legend of Arion.

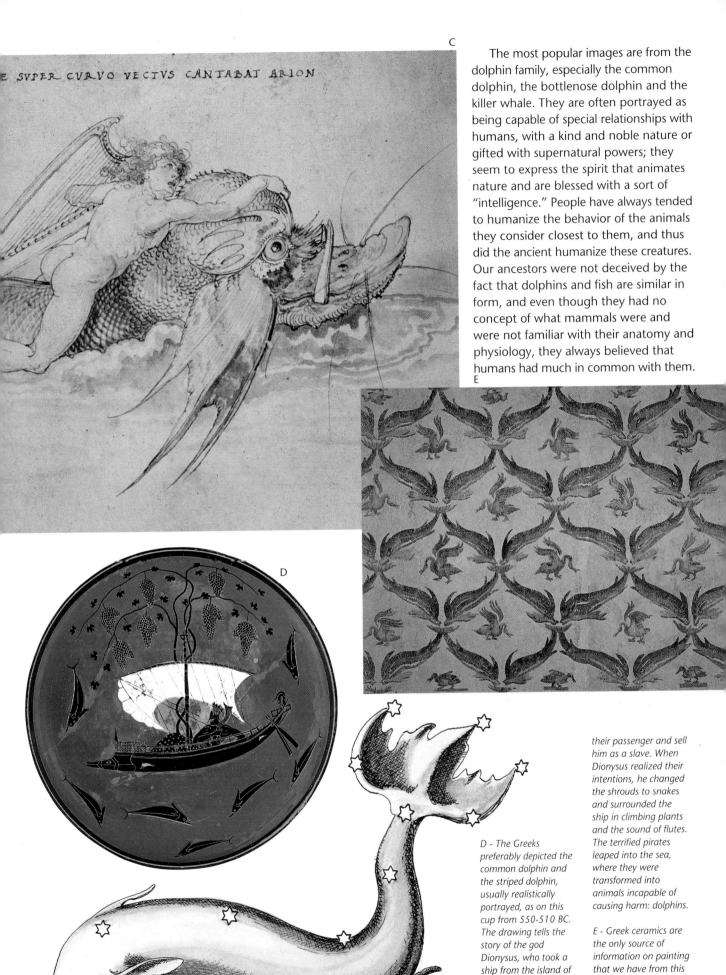

E SVPER CVRVO VECTVS CANTABAT ARION

C

The most popular images are from the dolphin family, especially the common dolphin, the bottlenose dolphin and the killer whale. They are often portrayed as being capable of special relationships with humans, with a kind and noble nature or gifted with supernatural powers; they seem to express the spirit that animates nature and are blessed with a sort of "intelligence." People have always tended to humanize the behavior of the animals they consider closest to them, and thus did the ancient humanize these creatures. Our ancestors were not deceived by the fact that dolphins and fish are similar in form, and even though they had no concept of what mammals were and were not familiar with their anatomy and physiology, they always believed that humans had much in common with them.

E

D

F

D - The Greeks preferably depicted the common dolphin and the striped dolphin, usually realistically portrayed, as on this cup from 550-510 BC. The drawing tells the story of the god Dionysus, who took a ship from the island of Ikaria to Naxos. As often occurred at that time, the crew was comprised of pirates who decided to kidnap

their passenger and sell him as a slave. When Dionysus realized their intentions, he changed the shrouds to snakes and surrounded the ship in climbing plants and the sound of flutes. The terrified pirates leaped into the sea, where they were transformed into animals incapable of causing harm: dolphins.

E - Greek ceramics are the only source of information on painting that we have from this era. Indeed, terra-cotta vases and mosaics have given us intact images of the splendid forms of dolphins.

9

A

But legends also serve to provide an explanation for things humans cannot understand. Here is how the Inuit explain the narwhal's unusual tooth.

A widow lived with a daughter and a blind son in an isolated hut made of whale bone, rocks and sealskin. A small window let in the sunlight. One day a polar bear (Nanuq) appeared at the window. Even though they had enough food, the woman forced her son to kill the bear, and helped him to take aim. Lying, she said that the animal had

escaped, but she dragged it away, cooked it and secretly ate it with her daughter. The daughter managed to hide some pieces of meat for her brother, who could thus eat while his mother slept. The winter passed and spring arrived. The blind boy asked his sister to accompany him to the seashore, to leave him there alone, and to make some stone markers (nukskuk) so he could find his way back. Two loons were swimming along the coast. One of them approached the boy and

had him climb upon its back, and then took him out to sea and immersed him in the water over and over until his sight was restored. When the boy returned home, he saw the bearskin and asked his mother where it had come from. Lying yet again, she said that it was a gift from some hunters. Summer came, and herds of white belugas passed by the camp. The boy prepared a harpoon with an old saw left by his father, some walrus tusks and the wood from an old whaling boat run

10

aground on the beach. He made a very sturdy line with sealskin, and using all this he caught enough belugas to have meat and maktak (blubber) for the whole winter. His greedy mother wanted him to hunt some more and tried to help him by holding the line to which the harpoon was attached. Two belugas emerged near them, and one of them was quite large. The woman told him to harpoon the smaller one, but the son missed his aim and hit the larger one, who dived into the water and dragged the woman down with it. When the whale reemerged, the mother was roped to its side. She cried out, "Udluk, udluk!" ("My knife!"). A whirlpool began to circle around her hair in a long spiral, and her hair transformed into a long tooth. The beluga dragged her to the bottom, where the two bodies united to become a narwhal. Even today, as hunters silently approach narwhals, they can hear the cry "Udluk, udluk!" before the animals dive under.

In China the river dolphin is known as the baiji, which means the color white. Chinese tradition often juxtaposed it with another odontocete common in fresh water and the estuaries of Southeast Asia, the finless porpoise, which is black. Despite its trusting behaviour, the baiji has never been portrayed as dolphins were in ancient Greece, or depicted by artists, who nevertheless were widely inspired by many aquatic creatures. The most ancient description of the baiji is found in a sort of dictionary known as "Erh Ya", of uncertain age (possibly around 1000 BC). The reason why the baiji and the finless porpoise are different in coulor is explained in this story:

In China there was a beautiful lake called Dong Ting. It was so beautiful that it looked like a painting. A lord named Bai lived there. He had a daughter as kind as she was beautiful, with white, delicate skin. This man was very strict and did not allow her to talk with anyone, but the girl was quite vivacious, and often secretly went to the shores of Dong Ting lake to play. There she met the young steward who had been hired the year before. They soon fell in love and began to meet on the beach, where the young man delighted the girl by playing a bamboo flute. One day, having heard the call of the flute, she set out for the beach, but was discovered by her father, who locked her in the house and ordered his servants to arrest the steward, and whip him. The girl ran to his aid, but overtaken by rage, her father drowned them both in Dong Ting lake. When the girl's mother learned of this, she drove her husband out of the house. Many years later, the man, who had become very rich, decided to return. On his way back, he raped a young singer voyaging on the same boat. In her grief, she committed suicide by throwing herself into the water. A sheet of paper then floated up to the surface, on which the following was written: "Many years ago you destroyed the love between your daughter and the steward by throwing them into the lake. Now you have led the daughter of another man to die in the same lake. You are a beast in human disguise." Suddenly a storm arose, the ship sank, and the man was changed into a dolphin with dark skin (the finless porpoise). When a dark dolphin is seen with a light dolphin, it is said that the father is following his daughter, transformed into a baiji.

B

A, B - It is certainly easy to invent a fantastic explanation for the narwhal's robust tusk. The male narwhal has two teeth in the upper jaw; the one on the left develops into a straight tusk in a sinistrorse spiral that can be as long as 3 m and weigh over 10 kg.

C - The baiji, on the origin of which a Chinese legend has been told in these pages, lives exclusively in the Yangtze river basin and is one of the species in the greatest danger of extinction.

C

There are many versions of every legend. As Calvino tells us, stories adapt to those who tell them and to the place and period, and we should listen carefully to made-up tales, because they always contain a grain of truth! The most recent experience shows that encounters between humans and dolphins are not only the stuff of fantasy and myth but have often based on real events.

The story of Old Tom is not a legend, although it sounds like one. At Twofold Bay on the southeast coast of Australia, whalers began to hunt the humpback whale and the southern right whale around 1830, continuing for a century. In the same area, the Australian aborigines had a different relationship with cetaceans for some time, in particular with killer whales. They believed that these whales were the reincarnation of dead warriors, and for this reason they offered food to the big cetaceans, who answered their calls.

In 1860 Alexander Davidson, a whaler, formed a crew of aborigines, intending to use their considerable skills as hunters. They kept on offering part of the whales killed to killer whales, who quickly learned to help the whalers in exchange for pieces of meat.

The men recognized each individual due to the scars they had on their skin or the form of their dorsal fins. The most well-known of the killer whales was a male called Old Tom, who seems to have helped the whalers in the bay for about 20 years. He was said to sometimes grab the line attached to the harpoon and drag the body of the dead whale to shore. He died of old age. On September 17, 1930 his body was recovered, and his skeleton is now at the Eden Museum near Sydney, Australia.

Today, in Shark Bay, Australia, dolphins regularly approach the coast to play and beg for food from swimmers. While this has become a great tourist attraction, if we were ancient Greeks,

A - According to the Bible, the first animal God created was the whale, a prodigious and powerful creature. The episode of Jonah, who was swallowed and then regurgitated, sparked the imagination of many painters. Here is an interpretation by Giotto (1266-1337), in the Cappella degli Scrovegni in Padua.

B - Jonah and the whale according to Sebastian Münster, a German geographer and cosmologist (1489-1552).

A

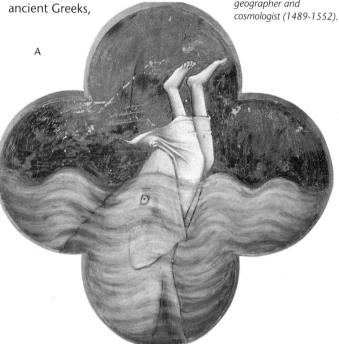

B

we would interpret this trust as a sign of benevolence from Poseidon.

Yet man cannot bear to be outdone by any other living creature on the planet, and while the collective imagination sees the dolphin as a friend that brings good luck, whales are too large and powerful for this. Thus, whale myths the world over express a dualism that includes the divine and the monstrous. The name itself, cetacean, which includes both whales and dolphins, comes from the Greek *ketos*, which means sea monster, who nevertheless is worthy of respect.

In *Moby Dick*, Melville says: "...the thought that this powerful monster is truly the crowned king of the sea will interest you..."

In the *Bible*, the book of Job tells us that Jonah is swallowed by the leviathan, which is undoubtedly a whale:

"Upon earth there is not his like, who is made without fear. He

C

River. When they were in his lodge, each wearing his own costume, they stood around the fire according to their rank and listened to his words. A long silence followed, then they all promised to respect his wishes forever. To show his gratitude, the chief decided to wear each of their costumes in turn. From that day on, the descendants of the great chief carve the images of sea monsters on the tops of their totem poles in his memory.

D

beholdeth all high things; he is a king over all the children of pride."

Islamic tradition also mentions whales, and says that a whale on the water holds up a bull who holds up an angel who carries the world on his shoulders. If the Devil distracts the whale and it moves, earthquakes are the result.

There are also legends, like this old Canadian story, which attempt to debunk the bad reputation that has always accompanied large animals:

Sea monsters were beings with supernatural powers who lived in a city on the bottom of the ocean. They captured people approaching in their canoes to fish. But one day, one of these fishermen, from the Haida tribe, was transformed into a killer whale and became their chief. The killer whale did not forget his origins and decided to convince the sea monsters not to attack fishermen anymore. He thus invited them to a great festival near the Nass

C - Legendary marine creatures are portrayed in this astrological map from 1660.

D - 16th-century mythology and legends are full of monsters. In this bestiary, the various species of whales and dolphins hold a place of honour. The Greek heroine Andromeda was saved by Perseus from a sea monster that was none other than a whale, as shown in Paolo Veronese's painting.

E - The animal caught, in the painting by Giulio Romano (1492-1546), could be a cetacean and if so this would demonstrate that this way of whaling was already common before the Japanese used it to hunt right whales in the 17th century.

E

THE BIRTH OF MODERN CETOLOGY

Although Greek fishermen had already sensed the affinity between humans and cetaceans, Aristotle (384-322 BC) was the first to affirm, in his *History of Animals,* that they were mammals and not fish. He had observed the differences in breathing, the fact that they had lungs and that they nursed their young. He also knew that there was a difference within this group of sea mammals, as some had teeth and others baleen, used to filter particles of food.

Authoritative writers of the past have described or mentioned whales; they include Virgil (70 BC-19 BC) in the *Æneid,* Plutarch (1st century), Aulus Gellius (2nd century) and Pliny the Elder (23-79 AD) in his *Historia Naturalis.*

Then, as with other sciences, in the Middle Ages reality was obscured and fantasy took over. Because of their large size, or perhaps because they had baleen instead of teeth, whales upset sailors and naturalists. Artists created singular representations of them, perhaps overly elaborating on the tales that inspired them. In medieval Scandinavia, whales must have been extremely important, as entire treatises were devoted to them and were probably used in instructing the king's children. In the 13th-century *Konungs*

A - It was the Swedish naturalist Carolus Linnaeus (1707-1778) who founded modern classification and introduced the binomial nomenclature.

B - The French naturalist Bernard Germain Etienne Lacépède (1756-1826) was commissioned by Buffon to complete his Natural Histroy *and his name is linked to the determination of the genera to which the white whale, bottlenose whale and fin whale belong.*

Skuggsja, or *Speculum Regalae* in Latin, whales are described as monsters with pointed teeth, crests and hooks. Even in the 1500's, numerous engravings show "whale-boars," "bearded whales" and so forth, representations which can be found in the *Historia Gentibus Septentrionalibus* (1555) by the Archbishop Olaus Magnus.

Yet this is when modern cetology was born, with Pierre Belon (1517-1564) in Paris, Ulisse Aldrovandi (1522-1605) in Bologna, and John Ray (1627-1705) in London.

Popular legends vanished as commercial whaling began. Books of legends were replaced by scientific treatises, and between the 18th and 19th centuries numerous writiers describe the habits and behaviour of whales in such an accurate manner that these works are still valid today, despite increased research in this area.

Some previously unknown species have been named after great scientists, primarily Carolus Linnaeus (1707-1778). In his *Systema Naturae*, he claimed that a classification for all animals was not just a convenience, but an acknowledgment that there are various levels of affinity that connect seemingly diverse animals. Bernard Lacépède (1756-1826) wrote the *Historie Naturelle des Cetacées*, which is

C - This oil painting by the Dutchman Esaias van de Velde immortalises the general curiosity aroused by a whale caught between Scheveningen and Katwa in January 1617.

D - Georges Cuvier (1769-1832) is portrayed here during a Comparative Anatomy lesson at the Museum of the Jardin des Plantes. He was the first to use the comparative method to reconstruct fossil mammals.

E, F, G - In the late 18th century, many scientists studied the anatomy and biology of these marine mammals. The plates show various species compared with each other, with details indicated. As in many drawings of the time, the animal's body appears rounded; this is because there were not many opportunities to observe them at sea, and they were often swollen or putrefied by the time they arrived in the laboratory.

E

F

G

H
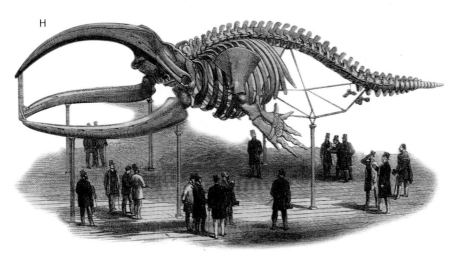

the most complete work of its time, and Georges Cuvier (1769-1832) published his *Historie Naturelle des Mammifères* in 1826.

Many researchers have given their names to new species discovered. Some of them include Philibert Commerson (1727-1773) for the Commerson's dolphin, and Daniel Esricht (1738-1863), a Danish cetologist who gave the gray whale its scientific name, *Esrichtius robustus*. Even today, scientists discover new species. For example, in 1991 three researchers, Reyes, Mead and van Waerebeek, identified and described *Mesoplodon peruvianus*, a new species of beaked whale that had never been seen before, despite its great size.

H - The 19th century was a time of great discoveries and unconditional faith in science. The establishment of many natural history museums throughout the world seems to confirm these certainties. A skeleton of a bowhead whale was exhibited at the Royal College of Surgeons in London.

WHALING

A

But despite the fact that dolphins were edible and tasty, no European nation ever made concentrated efforts to hunt them. Spain, France and Italy had adopted rules for dolphin kills, accompanied by cash prizes, but solely in the interests of sardine and anchovy fishermen.

Aside from these episodes, the age of cetacean hunting was based on whales, and over time it acquired a significance that went beyond the actual fact of whaling. Through whaling, new lands were discovered, relations with other civilizations began, wars and hostilities broke out, the customs and habits of entire populations changed, and traditions and certain ethnic groups became inextricably bound with the lives of the whales.

As whaling became popular, people stopped thinking of whales as monsters, because their flesh brought work, and sometimes even wealth.

Whales were hunted because they offered more product, but especially because they were slow, unlike the larger and faster rorquals. Small cetaceans were and in some cases still are hunted by some indigenous peoples, including the Inuit of Greenland, and fishermen in Indochina, the Philippines, Japan and the North Atlantic (Faer Øer).

Along the Mediterranean coast, dolphins were mostly considered helpers of man, and we have a great deal of information on the use of dolphins to spot migrating fish.

In a 1932 article, Police says that in the Bay of Naples there were two kinds of dolphins, the first known as bottlenose dolphins, who ate into fishermen's nets, damaging them irreparably, and the second, the common dolphin, who helped fishermen in their work by pushing fish into the nets. As a reward, they received bread soaked in wine. In the *Bollettino di Pesca, Piscicoltura e Idrobiologia*, again from 1932, Gustavo Brunelli indicates all the possible uses of the various species of dolphins in various coastal areas of Europe. Their meat was eaten and their bones used as fertilizer. In Spain, they were primarily used to make *carnada* bait when hunting sharks, while in Italy their meat was dried to make a product known as *mosciame*.

B

A, B, C - For centuries, whaling employed hundreds of thousands of men, using different techniques depending on culture and technology. At first, man and whale were almost at the same level, in a battle which either of them might win or lose. With the use of larger boats and technology, man's supremacy marked not only the decline of cetacean populations, but also the decline of whaling. The plates show various whaling scenes: an attempt to capture a bowhead whale (A), by James Steward (1791-1863); hunting a sperm whale (B), by James Steward; and hunting a whale from steamships (C) in the late 19th century.

Today, whaling's impact on the survival of cetaceans is the primary consideration, and not everyone knows that many everyday objects which are useful or even indispensable in our lives, were based on processing various parts of the whale's body; even today it is difficult to find basic products that have the same characteristics and can adequately replace those provided by these fascinating animals.

We need to distinguish two kinds of whaling. One involved a sort of romantic struggle in which man and animal were almost on an equal footing, in a battle in which either of them could emerge the victor. The second is signaled by the era of technology, steam ships and the undisputed supremacy of man. Yet old and new may exist side by side, and the advent of technology has not always spelled an end to old traditions. Even today some indigenous peoples engage in subsistence hunting, using supposedly "primitive" methods which are the result of empirical knowledge acquired over thousands of years. Until 1984, even the sperm whale was hunted according to traditional methods in the waters around the Azores. But let's take a step back in time.

The land around the Arctic Circle has always been inhospitable and unfit for agriculture, so primitive peoples of the North were forced to search for food in the sea. A whale offered much more than meat; it contained oil for lamps, bones for weapons, utensils, frameworks for doors and ceilings of huts, and its bladder and intestines were inflated to make buoys used in fishing.

The Norwegians practised whaling as early as the Neolithic, about 6000 years ago, and even today, engravings that date back to 2000 BC can be seen in Hammer, depicting fishermen pursuing a large animal blowing its spout.

In Greenland, ancient remains of villages built of whale bones have been found. The Mongols of the Sakhalin Islands off the coast of Japan hunted large cetaceans in kayaks, as did the inhabitants of the Aleutian Islands, who used poisoned arrows, causing the whale to die of blood poisoning.

This activity was not common only in northern peoples. Whaling boats in the Mediterranean are confirmed in Phoenician documents, as the Phoenicians had to pay tribute to their competitors, the Assyrians and Egyptians: "...The teeth of the blower, products of the sea, shall be given to you in tribute." On the other hand, the Greeks and Romans do not seem to have hunted cetaceans, and, as we have seen, had a deep respect for dolphins.

Hunting was thus an activity known to and practised by many peoples, but the information that has been passed down to us is fragmentary, and what has survived primarily regards regulations involving the transport of goods, tolls that had to be paid, and servitudes to be imposed, thus confirming the economic importance of this activity.

C

D

D - Dolphins are being hunted with rifles in this scene from Brittany, where they were accused of interfering with regular fishing activities.

Many monasteries were built when the Normans invaded northern France in the 7th century during the Carolingian era, creating a need for large amounts of readily available food as well as lamp oil, fat for lubricating, and more. Thus, the southern right whale was hunted as a source of raw materials. One of the customary dishes in the refectory of the Abbey of Saint-Denis was the meat of *Crassus piscis*, a term that meant cetaceans.

Many documents testify to the importance of this activity. A text entitled *Miracula Sancti Vedasti* (875) describes whaling, which the monks of the Pas-de-Calais monastery practiced systematically. The prior of Héauville imposed port fees on anyone doing business in these aquatic mammals, and an edict issued by the Administration of Saint-Étienne de Caen describes the activities of a whaling company at Dives-sur-Mer.

During the same period, around

A

A - In 17th century, whaling moved to the northeast Atlantic and the Barents Sea, off the coast of Greenland and Finland. The Basques came to Spitzbergen in the first half of the 17th century, but not until after the English and the Dutch, with whom they had to compete. Whaling Balaena mysticetus, or the bowhead whale, began in these waters and continued for over two centuries.

B, C - Killing a whale was an important event that involved the entire village. German, Dutch, Russian and Asiatic peoples obtained benefits and wealth as they used similar methods to utilize all parts of the animal killed. The pictures show two different scenes involving the exploitation of large marine mammals: processing a whale in the port of Antwerp (B) and killing a whale in the freezing waters of the Russian seas (C).

the year 1000, Icelanders and Norwegians also hunted the right whale, driving it into fjords and then closing off the exit with nets. The whales were then finished off with arrows dipped in the blood of previous victims, causing their death by infection within a few days.

According to several sources, the Vikings discovered America around the year 1000 by following whales, thus preceding Columbus' voyage to the New World by over 400 years.

As described in Albertus Magnus' *De Animalibus*, the Germans also hunted whales, pursuing them on small boats with a three men crew. Believing that whales were attracted by music, they brought drums and other percussion instruments with them. If the whale approached, they harpooned it and dragged it to shore.

The Basques who inhabited the Gulf of Guascogna were the first to organize whaling on a commercial level. During the Reign of Navarra, the city of San Sebastian was granted privileges in trading baleen. These privileges were extended to

Fuenterrabia in 1203, to Guetaria in 1204, and to Zarautz in 1227.

In less than a century, the Basques had so developed their techniques that they had no rival anywhere in northern Europe. They hunted the southern right whale, which was slow-moving and docile, easy to approach in small oar-driven boats, and, most importantly, floated after it was killed. They hunted in groups of small boats; when whales were sighted, everyone threw free-flying harpoons, unattached to the boat, at a single whale.

As reported by several authors, the Basques called the whale *sardako* because of its custom of living in pods, which also facilitated its capture. Whales were hunted near the coast, starting from the fall equinox in September and continuing throughout the winter. All parts of the animal were utilized. The blubber was used for lamp oil, as a lubricant and for painting, the bones were used in making soap, and baleen provided wool and fabric for clothing and furnishings, as well as an endless series of other objects, so that whaling soon became not only important, but indispensable for the lives of entire populations. Heavy trading developed between Spain and France.

Then as now, as the activity became successful, taxes were levied on it, and starting in 1268, upon arrival in the Port of Biarritz, whalers had to pay a tax on every whale caught.

In Guetaria it was customary to offer the king the first whale of the season. This custom continued unquestioned for over three centuries. Even under English rule, in 1270, Edward I asserted all whaling rights against the Basques. By the 15th century, right whales were becoming increasingly rare. The most obvious conclusion was that they were being overhunted.

On the contrary, a number of scholars believe that this hypothesis is eccessively simplistic and incorrect, because due to the techniques used, the number of whales killed never exceeded 100 animals per season, a paltry sum when compared to the numbers killed in more recent times. Indeed, the archives of Lekeitio reveal a total of 48 kills between 1517 and 1661.

A second hypothesis attributes the disappearance of whales from the gulf to climate changes that occurred during that period. This caused a change in the amount of food available to right whales, which is also confirmed by the contemporaneous drop in the number of cod and herring caught. A decrease in whales killed near the coast could also be the result of changes in hunting habits. As the Basques hunted whales only during the winter, they began to explore other areas so they could whale all year, desiring to earn more.

Whatever the reason, the Basques moved to the mid-Atlantic, and their ships had reached Scotland by the 14th century. They arrived at

A

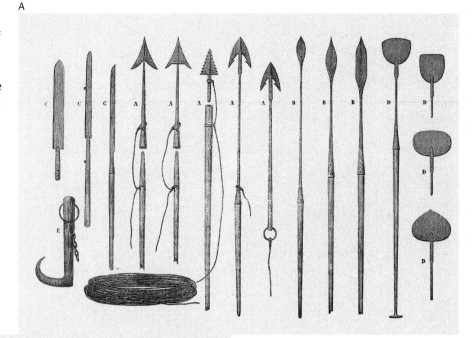

B

C

Groenfiord in the Gulf of Grunder in Iceland in 1412, with twenty vessels outfitted for whaling.

It was a short step from Iceland to America for these expert navigators, and a fascinating theory suggests that they came to the shores of America before Columbus. In fact, Branco's Atlas of 1436 shows a land far to the West called *Scorafixa* or *Stocafixa*, and other 15th-century maps also show islands which could be Newfoundland and are identified as *Bacalao*, a reference to the abundance of cod.

Nevertheless, the first documents that positively place the Basques on this island are dated 1550, where it is stated that the cities of Biarritz, Capbreton, Pasajes and San Sebastian outfitted whaling ships from Greenland and that cod fishing was practised in American waters.

Their number increased rapidly, and in 1570 at least fifty vessels were operating along the Labrador coast.

The Basques traded with indigenous peoples, especially the Eskimos, and shipped on foreign crews, teaching them their techniques, but saved for themselves the honour of carving up the dead animals.

In the late 16th century discord between France and Spain weakened their trading relationships, and around the same time Holland and England entered the competition for domination of the great maritime passages. These factors, plus the increasing rarity of whales along the American coasts, once again pushed the Basques to seek other areas to exploit in far-off, still unexplored seas. In 1600 whaling shifted to the eastern North Atlantic and the Barents Sea, off the coast of Greenland and Finland.

As they could not build land bases, they adopted new systems, inventing high seas hunting and on-board processing of blubber and meat.

The Basques arrived in Spitzbergen in the first half of the 17th century, after their English and Dutch competitors. In 1736 they obtained permission for exclusive whaling for 4 years, and in 1742, when their government suffered a number of political crises, they abandoned whaling. Nevertheless, as they were excellent sailors, they were shipped on as experts for whaling boats from other countries.

Concerning the English, in 1576 the Moscovy Company, established by Bristol shipowners, obtained a monopoly on whaling in the North Sea and the White Sea, which they maintained through the 1600's.

The first English expedition to Spitzbergen was in 1611. By 1786 they were capable of outfitting 162 ships to hunt right whales and bowhead whales in the Davis Strait. To understand the economic importance of this activity, suffice it to note that around 1750 the city of London owned 5000 streetlamps which functioned entirely on whale oil.Despite the numerous wars the English fought, which distracted them from whaling, and the constantly decreasing numbers of whales even during the first half of the 19th century, the English fleet was the largest in the whaling industry.

D

The most important figure during this period is undoubtedly William Scoresby (1789-1857).

The Dutch were not left behind. In 1596 a Dutch captain, Willem Barents, discovered Spitzbergen and in 1611 began building proper whale processing settlements. These great animals were hunted in light launches with a 6-man crew, with the harpoon attached to the boat. When the whale was harpooned, they allowed it to drag the boat until it tired, when it was finished off with lances. If it sank, it became difficult to recover, as it could sink the boat and the sailors could die from exposure.

The Noordsche Company was established in 1614 by the Chambers of Commerce of various Dutch cities in order to combat the English

monopoly. After various incidents caused by claimed rights to exclusive exploitation, in 1618 rules were established which divided exploitation of the waters around Spitzbergen among the Basques, the English and the Dutch. A year later the Dutch founded the city of Smeerenberg, which became a refuge and port of call for 18,000 whaling ships. In 1719 a reserve of bowhead whales was discovered in the Davis Strait, and these were also hunted. In 1770, Dutch whaling declined as a result of competition from the English and the beginning of whaling in America. The epoch of Dutch whaling ended around 1778. According to some documents, from 1669 to the time whaling ended, they had killed 64,576 right whales and bowhead whales.

A, B - The introduction of the harpoon launch marked a turning point in whaling methods. This engraving shows various types of harpoons. Whaling in the Azores was along different routes:

English whalers were the first to whale here. In a letter to the Queen in October 1768, the governor of the islands, D. Antao de Almada, notes the presence of 200 ships from New England, 250 barrels

of oil and 100 barrels of spermaceti from one season of whaling. In 19th century, American whalers also stopped at Fajal and Pico to load barrels of oil onto ships headed for America. In the early 1900's, all boats used were made

locally, and in 1909 the first motor boat for pulling launches was used. Whaling officially ended in 1984. The last three sperm whales were killed in 1987 to protest decisions by the International Whaling Commission.

C - The harpooner of the early 19th century was soon replaced.

D - Harpoon hunting required an almost direct contact with the whale. This 1880 painting shows a group of sperm whales trapped in a fjord in Iceland.

The whaling industry in America was started by the English as they settled new territories, although for centuries indigenous peoples had hunted whales from canoes.

By 1670, the port of Nantucket had become the greatest whaling center in America, and two centuries later, Captain Akab left this port on his last voyage in search of Moby Dick.

In 1712 Captain Christopher Hussey accidentally caught a sperm whale, a different species from that normally hunted.

The sperm whale is not a true whale. It has teeth and is powerful and fast, but its meat is more valuable, its oil lighter, its teeth are of ivory, its stomach contains ambergris, and its enormous head has a special organ, the spermaceti, which hardens when exposed to air.

Whalers quickly organized, and ships were equipped with boilers to process the animals killed. The fleet expanded rapidly after the *Betsey* of Dartmouth, the first whaling vessel thus equipped, and by 1774 there

A - American whaling began in the first half of the 18th century. In just a short time, the number of ports and ships rose dramatically. During the long period the vessel spent sailing the seas in search of whales, the ship commander would prepare detailed reports filled with valuable drawings, which for centuries had been the only source of information on whale species and distribution.

A

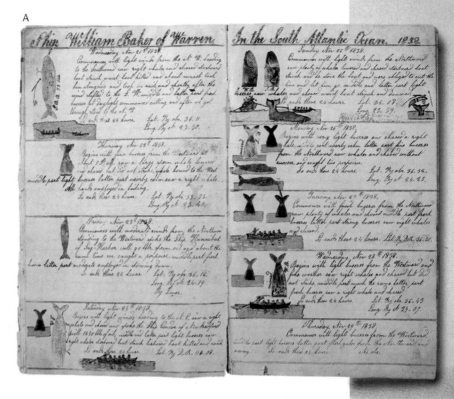

B

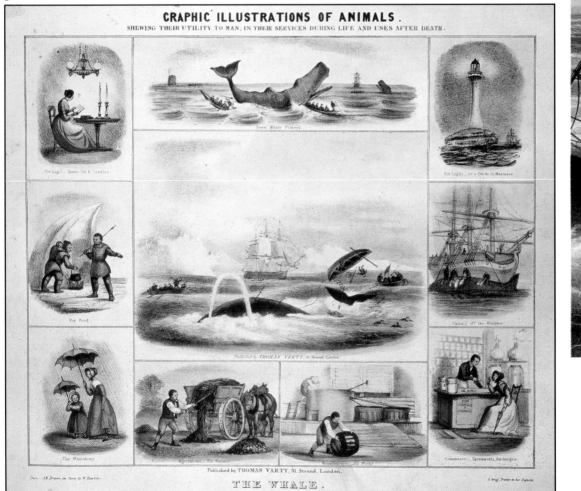

were 360 ships in New England, weighing a total of 33,000 tons and providing work for 4,700 sailors. Annual production reached 58,000 barrels of oil and spermaceti, and 33,750 kg of baleen. Between 1712 and 1761, whaling expanded from the Davis Strait to the Bahamas and from the West Indies to Africa, and the Antilles and South America were also explored in voyages that might last as long as five years.

In 1775 the Revolutionary War between England and the United States greatly damaged the whaling industry, and hunting continued only from Nantucket. After a period of decreased demand for products derived from right whales and sperm whales, trade recovered through new trade agreements. By 1807, Nantucket whalers were hunting in Brazil, off the coast of the Cape of Good Hope, in the Pacific and in Australia. The United States fleet expanded from 203 vessels in 1829 to 644 in 1844. Of these, 315 hunted sperm whales and 329 right whales. Two years later, the fleet consisted of 735 vessels that employed 70,000 persons; 254 ships were in operation in New Bedford alone. For a quarter of a century, the whaling industry created wealth, trade and prestige, providing a basis for the economic power of the United States.

Factories manufacturing harpoons, rigging and nails sprang up; the oil was exported to countries throughout the world to lubricate the machines created through the Industrial Revolution and illuminate large cities. Work multiplied, along with rich businessmen and shipowners and sailors of every race, from Azore islanders to Africans and Indians.

No one has described whaling during this period with more accuracy than Herman Melville in Moby Dick. Nevertheless, the epoch of whaling was drawing to a close.

The discovery of petroleum (1859) made it possible to substitute whale oil and its derivative products, but demand remained high, despite the fact that whales had become extremely rare.

B - In 1712, following a completely accidental capture, the commercial importance of a new species was discovered: the sperm whale. Thereafter, the whaling industry discovered new frontiers through products made from spermaceti and ambergris. A flourishing secondary industry sprang up that involved both the sea, with the training of sailors, the search for new navigation technologies, and the exploration of new lands, and all the land-based industries that processed the materials obtained from the sperm whale. The plate shows the various uses of products obtained from cetaceans.

C - When a ship left port, it might stay at sea for long periods and as time passed, whales had to be sought ever farther away. Often the ships remained at sea till their holds were full. This engraving shows whaling in the Antarctic.

A

B

A - The introduction of steamships and the harpoon-launching cannon improved whaling efficiency. In the photograph, skipper Duncan Greys poses with his harpoon-launching cannon, seventy kg of metal and a head full of explosive capable of reaching an animal 50 m away.

B - The harpoon-launching cannon made it possible to kill different species of whale, like the blue whale, which formerly had been impossible to hunt.

	1910	1911	1912	1913	1914	1915	1916	1917	1918	1919	1920	1921	1922	1923	1924	1925	1926	1927	1928
BLUE WHALE	316	704	1739	2417	2968	4527	5302	4351	2502	1993	2274	2987	5257	6869	4845	7548	7229	8722	9676
FIN WHALE	1303	2291	3169	6408	6168	5488	6432	3469	3413	4269	4946	6904	4494	6723	6894	9121	14288	8630	7203
HUMPBACK WHALE	5960	10750	12829	8997	7306	3217	2030	481	203	340	545	603	1162	1979	1206	3342	3050	2557	1526
WHALE*	801	704	57	616	725	730	495	647	1045	1040	1120	687	781	898	1719	1093	1494	1997	2290
SPERM WHALE	43	182	547	397	722	828	1012	385	909	1087	749	751	820	699	950	1439	1591	1316	1804
OTHERS**	3878	5777	6197	6838	5091	3530	2271	755	1396	1513	1735	242	1408	1052	1225	710	588	993	1094
TOTAL	12301	20408	24838	25673	22980	18320	17542	10088	9468	10242	11369	12174	13940	18120	16839	23253	28240	24215	23593

	1929	1930	1931	1932	1933	1934	1935	1936	1937	1938	1939	1940	1941	1942	1943	1944	1945	1946	1947
BLUE WHALE	13792	18755	29649	6705	19067	17486	16834	18108	14636	15035	14152	11550	5028	81	151	353	1111	3675	9382
FIN WHALE	9269	14303	11367	4158	7089	8734	14078	12155	17687	29680	22622	19722	9150	2169	1809	2204	2617	10984	16495
HUMPBACK WHALE	339	2035	923	635	501	2289	4088	7763	9854	5125	1393	454	2939	306	288	282	303	495	290
WHALE*	1549	841	652	492	433	541	962	823	1236	929	815	538	807	373	506	989	218	747	1131
SPERM WHALE	1862	1212	517	632	1234	1847	2238	4853	7055	3763	5511	4671	5641	4957	5503	2614	1669	3461	7546
OTHERS**	1179	666	21	366	583	1689	1111	1153	911	370	1290	769	73	128	115	3	1	22	56
TOTAL	27990	37812	43129	12988	28907	32586	39311	44855	51379	54902	45783	37709	23638	8014	8373	6445	5919	19384	34820

C

D

The development of technology put an end to traditional whaling. In 1863 Sven Foyn invented the harpoon-launching cannon, and sailboats were replaced by steamships, making it possible to hunt faster and larger new species like the blue whale. In 1868 the steam-powered whaling ship *Spes et Fides* took its maiden voyage, armed with a harpoon-launching cannon. In a single season it killed 30 rorquals. In 1885, 30 whaling ships killed 1,287 animals. New frontiers opened in whaling, and in 1904 the Norwegians built the Grytviken base on the island of South Georgia near the Antarctic land.

As World War I approached, and later on through World War II, whaling industry again expanded, especially in demand for glycerin, which was used to make explosives. During the two wars 50,000 whales were killed, an unthinkable number up to that time. As the Atlantic Ocean was a war zone, the Norwegians hunted along the more peaceful coasts of Chile and Peru.

The English then designed a new type of ship, the factory ship, which had an inclined surface to tip dead whales on board. This type of ship, which permitted greater autonomy, increased hunting in the Antarctic, especially the Ross Sea.

Prior to World War II, 21 factory ships operated in the Antarctic, owned by Norwegian, English, Dutch and Russian companies. At the end of the war, the whaling fleet was in a disastrous condition, but the need for food and other products was great, and in the name of democracy it was worth the effort to begin whaling again. From the 1950's to the early 1960's, the Antarctic was once again the scene of whaling that had never reached such epic proportions; once again, the protagonists were the Norwegians and the Russians, with the Japanese as new arrivals. Today, whaling continues as subsistence hunting is allowed for indigenous peoples and special permits are issued to Japanese and Norwegian ships for scientific purposes, with take limits set by the International Whaling Commission.

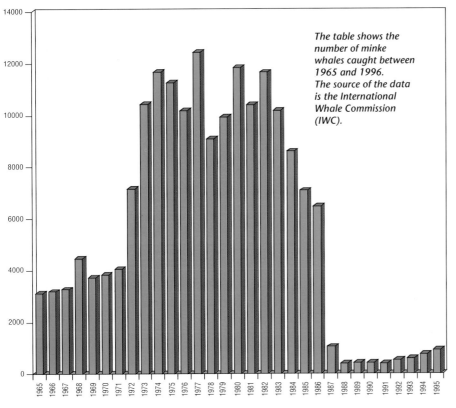

The table shows the number of minke whales caught between 1965 and 1996. The source of the data is the International Whale Commission (IWC).

	1948	1949	1950	1951	1952	1953	1954	1955	1956	1957	1958	1959	1960	1961	1962	1963	1964	1965	1966
BLUE WHALE	7157	7781	6313	7278	5436	4218	3009	2495	1987	1775	1966	1328	1067	1846	1103	1688	439	695	397
FIN WHALE	24028	21763	22902	22819	25605	25581	31335	32185	31496	31626	31587	30942	30985	31790	30178	21916	19182	12317	6882
HUMPBACK WHALE	515	3395	5063	4352	4023	3328	3155	2713	3880	3196	2923	5055	3576	2840	2436	2758	318	452	59
WHALE*	1573	1855	2471	3033	3123	2208	2491	1940	2076	3138	5670	5539	7035	7785	8804	9549	13690	25453	23067
SPERM WHALE	9850	9016	8186	18264	11557	9577	13543	15593	18590	19156	21846	21298	20344	21130	23316	27858	29255	25548	27378
OTHERS**	306	192	125	49	88	97	109	149	33	99	523	2328	7478	8974	7665	3061	5754	8006	7110
TOTAL	43431	44002	45060	55795	49832	45009	53642	55075	58062	58990	64515	66490	70845	74365	73502	66830	68638	72471	64893

	1967	1968	1969	1970	1971	1972	1973	1974	1975	1976	1977	1978	1979	1980	1981	1982	1983	1984	1985
BLUE WHALE	220	57	95	35	35	17	11	0	0	1	2	3	0	0	0	0	0	0	0
FIN WHALE	6458	5268	5320	5212	4547	4191	2657	2142	1552	741	310	711	730	472	410	356	278	281	219
HUMPBACK WHALE	4	2	9	15	24	6	19	16	17	15	20	35	19	18	12	16	16	15	8
WHALE*	19016	16960	12483	11561	11372	8804	7460	8121	6865	3651	3433	1623	1055	620	748	873	797	804	395
SPERM WHALE	26424	24080	23929	25521	22642	18558	22422	21421	21189	17353	12259	10971	8554	2092	1452	621	414	463	400
OTHERS**	7839	9567	7657	7484	5551	6840	213	205	189	211	216	198	194	199	152	170	179	180	180
TOTAL	59961	55934	49493	49828	44171	38416	32782	31905	29812	21972	16240	13541	10552	3401	2774	2036	1684	1743	1202

The table shows the data of the International Whale Commission regarding the number of whales, fin whales, sperm whales and other cetaceans caught between 1910 and 1986. The data for the 1957-1973 period have been updated on the basis of information gathered by the IWC in 1994 from the Russian Commissioners who indicated the real number of the catches made by their fleet.
* Until 1967-68 the term "fin whales" included the sei whale and in the following years included the Bryde's whale.
** The term "others" includes different species of cetaceans and since 1957 it can also include specimens of species indicated in the other columns with the exception of the blue whale.

C - In the Azores, sperm whales were killed predominantly, especially in Pico isle which is represented in this photo.

D - With the new power of technology, new frontiers in whaling opened up. In 1904, the Norwegians built the Grytviken base on the island of South Georgia, near Antarctica. From the 1950's to the early 1960's, the Antarctic was the scene of whaling on a massive scale never before witnessed. Once again, the protagonists were the Norwegians, the Russians and the Japanese. In 1962, they killed 73,502 whales in a single season.

E, F, G - In the early 20th century, the Norwegians built the first factory ships capable of sailing great distances and performing most work on board. All whaling nations then copied these ships.

PROTECTIVE MEASURES

The first regulations were adopted in the early 1900's. The growth of modern civilization and the consequent industrial development had a negative impact on the environment, and whaling is one of its most emblematic cases. As they live in the open sea, whales were and are considered the property of anyone, and thus a resource free from any regulation. Moreover, as they provided some of the products necessary for industrial development, no one had either the ability or the desire to consider the effects of excessive exploitation of an abundant, renewable, but not inexhaustible, resource.

Industrial hunting techniques have exerted such pressure on populations of some species of rorquals that they have been brought to the edge of extinction. This fact was not understood over the short term, because upon the exhaustion of one population, other were sought out, perhaps of different species, widening the range of action.

Whaling expanded so rapidly that by the 1930's, 85% of world catches took place in almost all waters of the Antarctic. In 1938, 54,902 whales of different species were killed, 95% taken by the Norwegians and English.

Due to conflicts with coastal fishing, Norway prohibited hunting in territorial waters starting in 1904, and from 1915-1925 the prohibition extended to the Iceland Sea.

As problems arose in maintaining prices of whaling industry products, indiscriminate hunting was put to a stop. In 1927, the International Council for the Exploration of the Sea (ICES) attempted to regulate whaling and established a central organism for the purpose of collecting data on catches. Nevertheless, the first regulations were not definitive and only prohibited the killing of females who were pregnant or accompanied by calves; as late as 1931 these agreements had produced no results, both because they were inherently ineffective and most nations who practised whaling ignored them. Decreased earnings had more effect than the need to protect whales, and from 1930-31, following a surplus production of whale oil, which had by now reached 3.6 million barrels, prices dropped drastically, and whaling companies

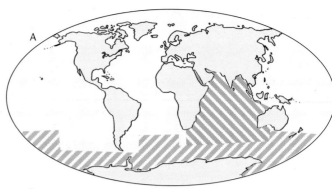

A - The IWC declared the portion north of the 55th parallel of the Indian Ocean a reserve in 1979. In 1992 such a disposition became permanent. Since 1994 the IWC has founded a sanctuary in the southern ocean south of the 40th parallel. Hunting in this zone is only allowed for research.

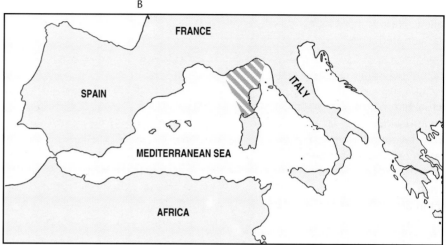

operating in the Antarctic decided to control hunting more efficiently.

As the goal was to gain economic control over production to ensure stable oil prices on the market, management techniques were introduced which did not consider the actual conditions of the population being hunted. The unit of reference was the amount of oil produced by a blue whale, which was the equivalent of two common rorquals, two and a half humpback whales or six right whales. After the continued failure of ICES agreements, in 1946 President Truman organized a conference that led to the creation of the International Convention for the Regulation of Whaling (ICRW), formed of fifteen signatory countries, all involved in the whaling industry. The objective of this organization was to conserve whales and more coherently develop the whaling industry. For this purpose, in that same year the ICRW created the International Whaling Commission (IWC), a control organ that even today meets every year to examine the actual application of the regulations passed. The agreement which led to the establishment of the IWC was signed in Washington, D.C. on December 2, 1946. Membership in the Commission

is open to all countries who formally adhere to the Washington convention. At the time of establishment, there were forty members. Each country is represented by a commissioner who may be assisted by experts. Commission headquarters are in Cambridge, England. Rules are discussed during annual meetings and can be passed with a vote of at least three quarters of those voting, and become effective ninety days later. These rules are not completely binding. Suffice it to note that if a member nation objects within ninety days, it can refuse to comply with the rule. The same thing happens if a government decides that these decisions limit its sovereignty.

In 1956 the IWC took its first step to a more protective approach, declaring that "...It is in the world's interests to protect the great natural resource represented by whales for future generations......as the history of the whaling industry has been to overhunt various areas one after another and to hunt to extinction one species after another." Thus, the purely commercial view of managing these resources was overcome. Nevertheless, the road to complete protection was long and difficult. Under pressure from whaling company interests in the 1950's and

1960's, unsustainable quotas from hunted populations were once again approved despite the observations of the Scientific Committee, which recommended quotas which could be sustained by reproduction rates and were consistent with estimated abundance. In 1960-61, 74,365 whales were killed, more than any other time in history. In the 1960's, England, the Netherlands and Norway stopped exploiting the Antarctic. In 1975 the so-called "New Management Procedure" was adopted, based on an established catch level which did not exceed what the population could sustain, but because there was no data on the actual numbers of many populations, it was decided to proceed by trial and error, favouring the interests of one nation or those of another.

In 1978 Pelli introduced an amendment to the Protective Fishery Act in the United States, providing economic sanctions against those who refused to follow the recommendations

C

D

of the IWC. During the same period, many non-governmental organizations sprang up that began massive anti-whaling campaigns. The most famous of these is Greenpeace, which has engaged in a public awareness campaign for many years.

In 1982 it was decided by majority vote to completely suspend hunting, accompanied by international prohibitions that outlawed trade in whale meat. Quotas were set at zero for deep sea hunting beginning with the 1985-86 Antarctic whaling season, and in 1986 for coastal whaling. Following this decision, the Scientific Committee decided to begin research which would make it possible to evaluate the status and dynamics of all large cetacean populations (Comprehensive Assessment), and to study a procedure for more effective management (Revised Management Procedure) that could replace the one adopted in 1975. The purpose was to continue exploiting stocks, keeping their populations at 72% of the initial level. A total ban was impossible for certain indigenous peoples: dolphins and other toothed whales are still hunted by the Inuit of Greenland and fishermen in Indochina, the Philippines, Japan and the North Atlantic (Faer Øer), who can continue to hunt at the subsistence levels established by the Commission.

In response to disputes among nations who want to continue whaling and the environmental concerns voiced by other countries, members of the IWC not directly involved in whaling, the governments of the Faer Øer Islands, Greenland (Denmark), Norway and Iceland established the North Atlantic Marine Mammals Commission (NAMMCO) in 1972, to coordinate research and exploitation of small cetaceans and pinnipeds. Norway and Japan have continued to whale throughout these years based on permits that allow whaling for scientific purposes. This has provoked strong

reactions from environmental associations.

The revelation that the statistics provided by commissioners from the former Soviet Union were falsified caused quite an outcry and showed how extremely difficult it can be to control and regulate this activity simply based on the number of individuals killed. In any event, these revelations provided a new view of the massacre that took place in the years following World War II up to 1986.

The IWC is also authorized to designate protected areas, and the first sanctuary was established in Antarctica south of the 40th parallel. In 1979 the Indian Ocean was also designated a full reserve, with the southern boundary at the 55th parallel; here, with the support of all coastal nations whether or not they are members of the Commission, any kind of commercial hunting is prohibited. While this decision was at first declared temporary, in 1992 it became permanent.

In 1993 the French government proposed extending the Antarctic sanctuary to the entire southern hemisphere south of the 40th parallel, and this resolution was permanently adopted in 1994.

The IWC has also recognized the agreement signed in Brussels on March 22, 1993 by France, Italy and the Principality of Monaco to establish a sanctuary in the Ligurian Sea in the Mediterranean, to protect the feeding areas of rorquals and to limit accidental kills of cetaceans by floating nets. The annual meeting of the International Whaling Commission was held in Monte Carlo in the Principality of Monaco in October 1997. At that time, the Irish commissioner proposed creating a global sanctuary in all waters of the world outside national jurisdictions, to prohibit international trade in whale products, to make controls more efficient and to stop hunting for scientific purposes.

B - On 22 March, 1993, in Brussels, Italy, France, and the Principality of Monaco signed an agreement on the institution of a sanctuary in the sea of Corsica, Liguria and Provence, with the aim to protect all the species of marine mammals. Despite the fact that this project has not been put into operation yet, as a result it limited fishing with drifting nets, and helped the development of public awareness about protection of cetaceans.

C - The Japanese built their fleet after World War II, with enormous units of 20,000-50,000 tons, capable of butchering whales killed and performing the first part of industrial production processes. The image shows a whale being lifted onto a whaling ship.

D - In the early 1900's, a campaign to protect whales slowly developed, with environmental associations, especially Greenpeace, playing a fundamental role. The photograph shows a demonstration performed by its members opposing to a whaling ship.

RETURN TO THE SEA

Despite some inconsistencies and cinematographic excesses, the success of films like *Jurassic Park* and *Waterworld* have made it possible for the public at large to gain familiarity with terms and concepts like evolution, geologic periods, genetics, mutation, and extinction.

Nature proceeds by trial and error, and the French botanists and zoologist Jean Baptiste Lamarck (1744-1829), who was the father of evolutionary theory, asserted that the surrounding environment stimulates changes in living forms. In other words, the giraffe has a long neck because feeding on the leaves of trees has caused it to more fully develop the use of this part of its body.

had to adjust to the new environment. Lamarck probably would have responded that he had developed gills because he was forced to dive underwater for food.

To Darwin, gills were simply a random malformation that under those particular circumstances made that man more efficient and better adapted.

Following some recent discoveries, Lamarck's ideas are being reexamined after years of unquestioned adherence to Darwinian theory. We will not delve into the question of whether the mutation was caused by selection or whether it was induced; the end result was that the star of *Waterworld* could breathe underwater, and over the long course of history, more or less similar adaptations have actually occurred.

which use special horny plates known as baleen, instead of teeth.

Paleontology is the science that examines evolutionary processes through the discovery and study of fossils; it attempts to decipher all clues a few bones found in the earth have preserved and can tell us.

The fragmentary nature of paleontological documentation does not permit a complete understanding of whether the processes of transformation we have spoken of begin with simpler forms and lead to more complex ones, or whether life expresses itself independently in a variety of trials and errors, only a few of which are successful.

In recent years biochemists, embryologists and geneticists have joined paleontologists, using new

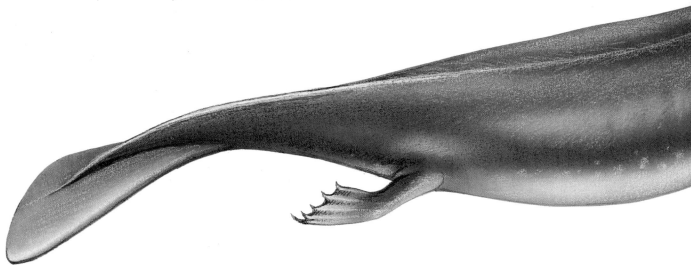

Subsequently, Alfred Wallace (1823-1913), although less known to the public, and Charles Darwin (1809-1882), gained permanent recognition for the theory of evolution.

Unlike Lamarck, Darwin stated that "...the life of animals is a continuous struggle for survival, where the weaker or less perfectly organized must always succumb." That is, present-day living beings are the product of a slow transformation from pre-existing forms; random mutations of their genetic heritage and natural selection have permitted them to survive and thrive.

Why did the star of *Waterworld* have gills? The world had been covered by water, and to adapt, man

The evolution of whales and dolphins, for example, is a rather singular affair. After some mammals conquered terra firma, the cetaceans returned to the sea, and they look more like fish than their terrestrial cousins. Certainly, it is difficult to believe that there is any similarity between a furry, four-legged creature and the tapered, smooth body of a dolphin, but their anatomy, physiology and embryology are unequivocally mammalian.

At present, the Cetacea order includes three suborders: Archaeoceti (the zeuglodonts), primitive cetaceans which are completely extinct; Odontocetes (toothed whales), cetaceans with teeth; and Mysticetes (baleen whales), cetaceans

investigation methods to complete the evolutionary history of the cetaceans. Nevertheless, despite much research, this history has many uncertain areas that are still subject to debate and disagreement.

In the Triassic period, 250 million years ago, the land above water looked much different than it does today. The seven continents as we now know them were grouped into two large masses of land, the continent of Gondwana in the south and the continent of Laurasia in the north. Everything else was covered by a single ocean. Temperatures were warm even at the poles, while the land above sea level was shaken by enormous volcanic eruptions. This is the time of the dinosaurs' undisputed rule. They were perfectly adapted for life in such a climate and they must have had very few real enemies. About 135 million years ago, Gondwana began to break up, forming Africa, South America, the Antarctic and India. Laurasia broke up into North America and Eurasia. The most overwhelming result of continental drift was the change in climate.

A - About 60 - 50 million years ago, a group of terrestrial mammals began to colonize the sea. The adaptation was gradual and some evolutionary attempts proved to be unsuitable and the animals became extinct. Among the completely adapted species to the aquatic surroundings the oldest are the Protocetides which belong to the order of the Archeocetes.

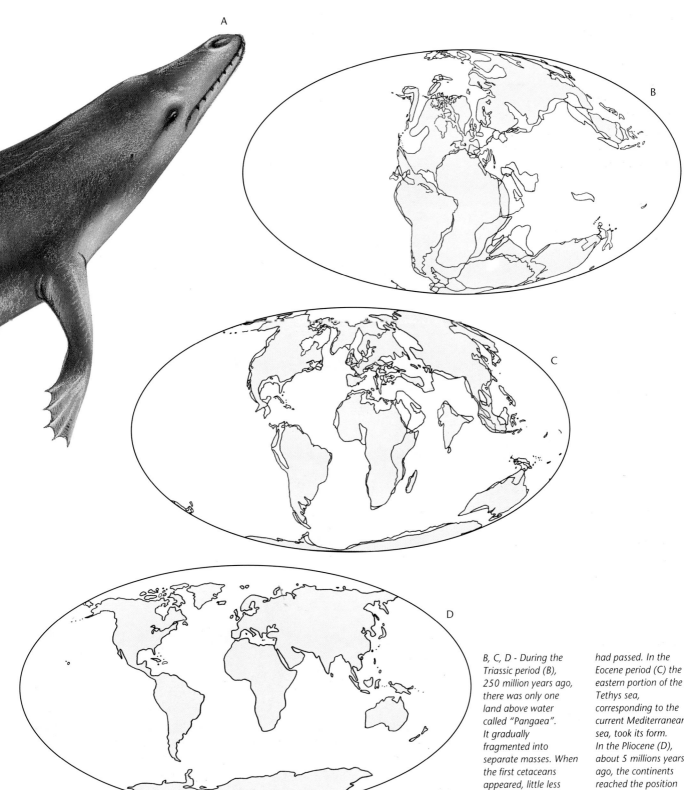

B, C, D - During the Triassic period (B), 250 million years ago, there was only one land above water called "Pangaea". It gradually fragmented into separate masses. When the first cetaceans appeared, little less than 200 million years had passed. In the Eocene period (C) the eastern portion of the Tethys sea, corresponding to the current Mediterranean sea, took its form. In the Pliocene (D), about 5 millions years ago, the continents reached the position currently known.

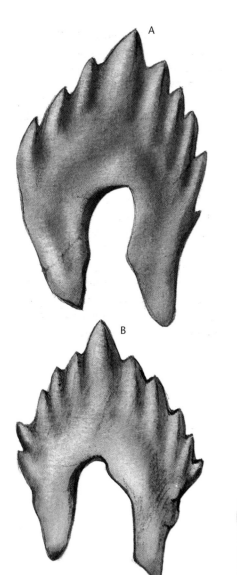

A

B

C

D

In reality, there are no precise reasons for this phenomenon, but probably the increase in volcanic activity, the consequent decrease in carbon dioxide in the atmosphere and the isolation of the continents played a fundamental role in the fall of temperatures. The Cretaceous period marked the decline of the age of the dinosaurs, and even today scientists debate whether they disappeared because it was colder, because a meteorite collided with the Earth, because of competition from mammals, or for all of these reasons and more.

The processes of nature are long and difficult to comprehend, especially if we compare them to the history of humans on the Earth. After 100 million years of undisputed rule, the dinosaurs stepped down, but they would only vanish for good 10 million years later!

Mammals quickly became predominant, and it is interesting to note several differences between the two groups. The dinosaurs dominated the world on two large continents, while mammals had to colonize a variety of environments, due to the separation of the lands above water, and had to assume forms and adapt in ways the dinosaurs never succeeded in doing. Moreover, the progenitors of sea lions, fur seals, dugongs and cetaceans abandoned land to live in the sea, repeating what many species of reptiles had done prior to them.

The origin of cetaceans dates back to about 65 million years ago, while the oldest fossil discovery identified as a true cetacean was found in the rocks of the middle Eocene, dating to 55 million years ago.

Discoveries have been made in North Africa and in Asia and between India and Pakistan. This has led researchers to believe that they evolved on the shores of the Tethys Sea, which during that period stretched as far as the shores of Africa and India. As the continents drifted, the Tethys shrank considerably, and now one of its remnants is the Mediterranean Sea.

The study of the phylogenesis of cetaceans is a relatively modern

A, B, C, D - The discovery of fossil teeth represents an extremely important source of information: from these fossils it is possible not only to determine similarities among the various species but also to understand what they ate. Unlike contemporary Odontocetes, the Archeocetes had heterodont dentition; the molars and pre-molars were pointed (A, B, C) while the other teeth were conical (D). This type of dentition was very similar to that of the Mesonychids, terrestrial animals which lived along the coasts of the Tethys sea and fed on fish.

E - The Ambulocetus natans *represents the connection link between the real and proper cetaceans and the terrestrial ancestors. The skeleton of this animal, found in Pakistan and dated 52 million years, reveals its capability to move both on ground as well as in water. Probably it had webbed feet and it swam with dorsoventral movements of its body and its long tail.*

F - The Mesonyx *was probably one metre and a half long and had a very big head: its strong jaws indicate that it was a predator even though it belonged to the group of the Condylarthra, hoofed mammals from which there will derive the evolutionary lines which will lead to present-day camels and horses which are herbivorous.*

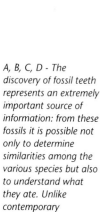

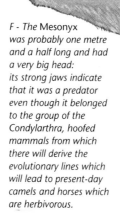

science, and only during the last century have several interpretations been provided, which scientists are still developing.

A comparison of fossil remains is not always enough to lead us back to the ancestors of today's whales and dolphins and determine their phylogenesis. Other methods, such as the comparison of proteins in the blood of marine mammals with those in land mammals, have made it possible to make further analogies.

In 1950, Alan Boyden and Douglas Gemeroy, researchers at Rutgers University, discovered a great similarity between cetaceans and ungulates, a class that includes camels, cows and horses. More recently, Vincent Sarich and Jerold Lowenstein used a more in-depth study of individual proteins to find albumin, and proved a close relationship between cetaceans and the hippopotamus.

The analogy in the protein composition of blood confirms other similarities between these two orders; both have a stomach divided into chambers, and the bone of the cranium, like the teeth, of primitive cetaceans, is similar to that of the first ungulates.

The common progenitor may belong to the Condylarthra order, which includes land animals which are primarily herbivores with plantigrade 5-toed clawed feet. They begin the evolutionary lines that gave rise to horses, camels, bison, giraffes, hippopotamuses and probably cetaceans.

A group in the Condylarthra order, the Mesonychidae, lived on the banks of the Tethys Sea at the end of the Paleocene and during the early Eocene, about 65 million years ago. Some were herbivores, but others were sarcophagous and active carnivores. In particular, *Mesonyx* looked like a large, hairy dog, and as the environment must not have been very hospitable, it fed on fish it caught in the water. The mesonychids were in all probability the ancestors of the archaeocetes, which, as we have noted, were true cetaceans.

The link between mesonychids and archaeocetes seems to have been an animal found in the sediment of Pakistan, datable to 52 million years ago and known as *Ambulocetus natans*; it was adapted to life in the water but could still move about on dry land. Its skeleton has many features which make it similar to both mesonychids and archaeocetes.

Ambulocetus swam by paddling with its back legs, using dorsoventral undulations of the spinal cord and its long tail, as can be seen in the particular form of its lumbar vertebrae. On dry land, it moved in a manner reminiscent of sea lions and seals.

So these animals were still primitive compared with present-day cetaceans, as they had not yet perfected the adaptations necessary for permanent life in the water.

For a long time the main family of archaeocetes, the Protocetidae, the closest descendants of the mesonychids, were known only through the discovery of a few fragments. But in 1964, on the island of Sheppey in England, the shoulder blade of an animal known as *Anglocetus* was found; more complete remains of a specimen known as *Pappocetus lugardi* were discovered in Nigeria; and finally, *Protocetus atavus* was found in Egypt. This small animal still had articulated sacral vertebrae with pelvic bones, vestiges of a land progenitor. The features which most distinguish these fossil finds is the form of the teeth, which is still extremely variable and suggests various levels of adaptation to the new availability of food in the water.

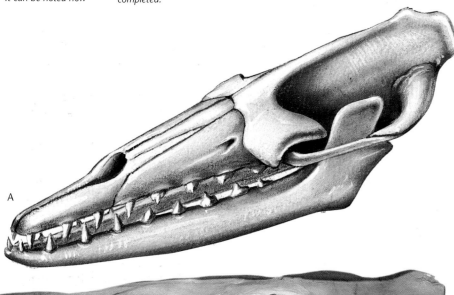

A

B

C

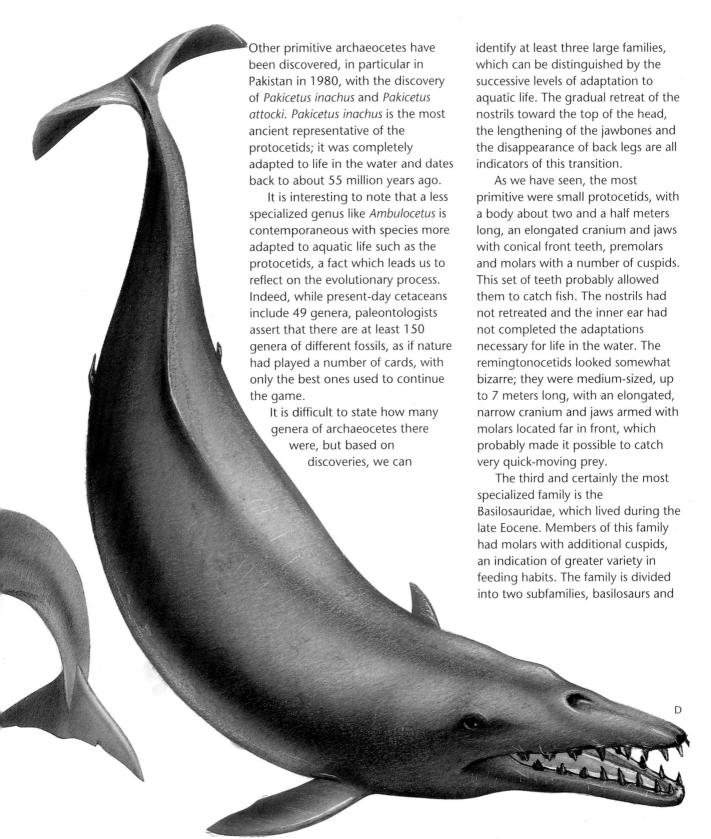

Other primitive archaeocetes have been discovered, in particular in Pakistan in 1980, with the discovery of *Pakicetus inachus* and *Pakicetus attocki*. *Pakicetus inachus* is the most ancient representative of the protocetids; it was completely adapted to life in the water and dates back to about 55 million years ago.

It is interesting to note that a less specialized genus like *Ambulocetus* is contemporaneous with species more adapted to aquatic life such as the protocetids, a fact which leads us to reflect on the evolutionary process. Indeed, while present-day cetaceans include 49 genera, paleontologists assert that there are at least 150 genera of different fossils, as if nature had played a number of cards, with only the best ones used to continue the game.

It is difficult to state how many genera of archaeocetes there were, but based on discoveries, we can identify at least three large families, which can be distinguished by the successive levels of adaptation to aquatic life. The gradual retreat of the nostrils toward the top of the head, the lengthening of the jawbones and the disappearance of back legs are all indicators of this transition.

As we have seen, the most primitive were small protocetids, with a body about two and a half meters long, an elongated cranium and jaws with conical front teeth, premolars and molars with a number of cuspids. This set of teeth probably allowed them to catch fish. The nostrils had not retreated and the inner ear had not completed the adaptations necessary for life in the water. The remingtonocetids looked somewhat bizarre; they were medium-sized, up to 7 meters long, with an elongated, narrow cranium and jaws armed with molars located far in front, which probably made it possible to catch very quick-moving prey.

The third and certainly the most specialized family is the Basilosauridae, which lived during the late Eocene. Members of this family had molars with additional cuspids, an indication of greater variety in feeding habits. The family is divided into two subfamilies, basilosaurs and

C, D - The order of the Archeocetae was composed by Protocetidae, Remingtonocetidae and Basilosauridae, these last were probably the most specialised group. Some palaeontologists retain that these could be divided in two sub-groups: Basilosaurinae and Durodontinae. To the first group there belong long-bodied species, with bodies even 20 metres long like Basilosaurus isis and Basilosaurus cetoides (C), to the second group species with more compressed vertebra like Durodon osiris and Zygorhyza kochii (D). It is believed that the present day cetaceans derive from the Durodonti.

durodonts. In the first, with members like *Basilosaurus cetoides*, the vertebrae were quite elongated, with a body that could be 20 meters long; the cranium was rather small, only a meter long. Durodonts like *Zygorhyza kochii* had shorter vertebrae and strong teeth.

Adaptation was not yet complete, and traces of their life on land persist, including small but well-defined back legs. The archaeocetes specialized quite rapidly, in "only" twenty or thirty million years.

All these fossils have teeth which include incisors, canines and molars, while present-day odontocetes are the only mammals which are homodonts, i.e. they have only one form of tooth. Present-day mysticetes use baleen rather than teeth, which facilitates filtering the small marine organisms on which they feed. On the contrary, primitive mysticetes had teeth.

The transition from more or less complete teeth to baleen took place early on and resulted in profound changes in the structure of the cranium. In particular, the jawbones transformed into an elongated plate on which the horny laminae that make up baleen could be suspended.

The cetoterids were one of the first mysticetes with this characteristic, similar to present-day rorquals. They appeared between the end of the Eocene and the beginning of the Oligocene, about 34 million years ago.

It is assumed that the odondocetes evolved from durodont basilosaurs. During evolution, the cranium underwent profound transformations, becoming larger, with completely retreated nostrils shifting up to its raised apex, while the asymmetry of the left and right sides increased and the bone surrounding the ear shifted away from the walls. The jaws are significantly elongated. The teeth have changed from different forms to a single triangular, conical shape. In some species they may even be absent or almost non-functional.

This evolutionary path to modern cetaceans suggests that archaeocetes were an intermediate form. While this theory is the most widely accepted, it is still only one of the hypotheses on their origin. In reality, it is possible that the archaeocetes were an evolutionary attempt which proved to be unworkable and that they became extinct without leaving any descendants. Moreover, fossil finds have left us messages that can be interpreted in many different ways.

The *polyphyletic* theory holds that odontocetes, mysticetes and archaeocetes have different origins.

This theory places great importance on differences in the cranium, probably due to different

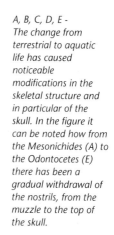

A, B, C, D, E - The change from terrestrial to aquatic life has caused noticeable modifications in the skeletal structure and in particular of the skull. In the figure it can be noted how from the Mesonichides (A) to the Odontocetes (E) there has been a gradual withdrawal of the nostrils, from the muzzle to the top of the skull.

The intermediate Protocetidae (B) and Basilsauridae (C) still have nostrils on the rostrum, while the change in the carnivorous Sharks (D) is practically complete. The skull initially pressed sideways widens. The jaws and the forejaws, besides lengthening frontwards, expand covering the frontal bones and surrounding the nostrils.

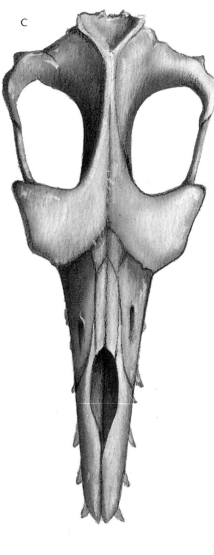

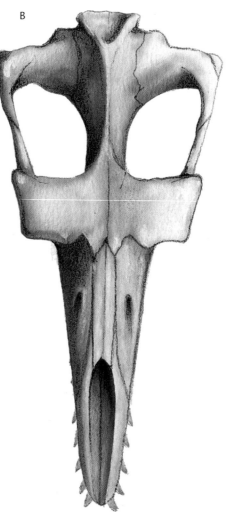

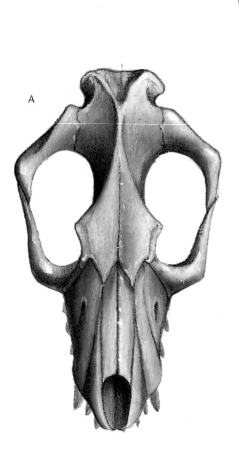

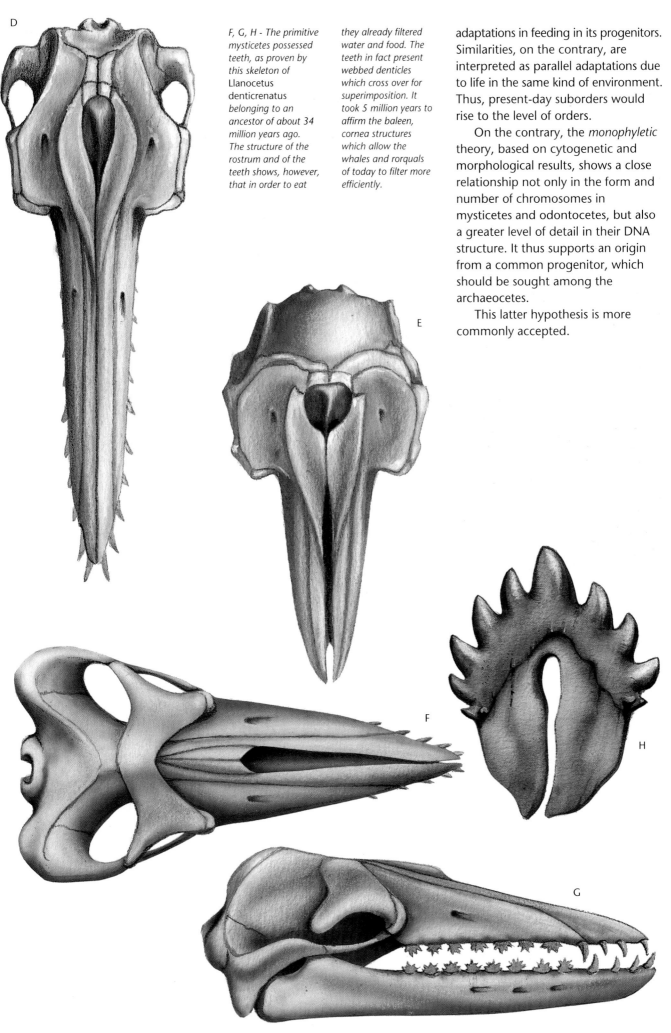

D

F, G, H *- The primitive mysticetes possessed teeth, as proven by this skeleton of Llanocetus denticrenatus belonging to an ancestor of about 34 million years ago. The structure of the rostrum and of the teeth shows, however, that in order to eat they already filtered water and food. The teeth in fact present webbed denticles which cross over for superimposition. It took 5 million years to affirm the baleen, cornea structures which allow the whales and rorquals of today to filter more efficiently.*

adaptations in feeding in its progenitors. Similarities, on the contrary, are interpreted as parallel adaptations due to life in the same kind of environment. Thus, present-day suborders would rise to the level of orders.

On the contrary, the *monophyletic* theory, based on cytogenetic and morphological results, shows a close relationship not only in the form and number of chromosomes in mysticetes and odontocetes, but also a greater level of detail in their DNA structure. It thus supports an origin from a common progenitor, which should be sought among the archaeocetes.

This latter hypothesis is more commonly accepted.

E

F

H

G

CETACEANS

ODONTOCETES

PHYSETERIDAE

PHYSETER

Physeter catodon
Sperm whale

KOGIA

Kogia breviceps
Pygmy sperm whale

Kogia simus
Dwarf sperm whale

MONODONTIDAE

DELPHINAPTERUS

Delphinapterus leucas
Beluga

MONODON

Monodon monoceros
Narwhal

ORCAELLA

Orcaella brevirostris
Irrawaddy dolphin

ZIPHIIDAE

BERARDIUS

Berardius bairdi
Baird's beaked whale

Berardius arnuxi
Arnoux's beaked whale

HYPEROODON

Hyperoodon ampullatus
Northern bottlenose whal

Hyperoodon planifrons
Southern bottlenose whale

MESOPLODON

Mesoplodon bahamondi
Bahamond's
beaked whale

Mesoplodon bidens
Sowerby's beaked whale

Mesoplodon bowdoini
Andrew's beaked whale

Mesoplodon carlhubbsi
Hubbs's beaked whale

Mesoplodon densirostris
Blainville's
beaked whale

Mesoplodon europaeus
Gervais's beaked whale

Mesoplodon ginkgodens
Ginkgo-toothed
beaked whale

Mesoplodon grayi
Gray's beaked whale

Mesoplodon hectori
Hector's beaked whaler

Mesoplodon layardi
Mesoplodonte di Layard

Mesoplodon mirus
True's beaked whale

Mesoplodon pacificus
Longman's beaked whale

Mesoplodon peruvianus
Pygmy beaked whale

Mesoplodon stejnegeri
Stejneger's beaked whale

Mesoplodon sp.
Mesoplodon species

TASMACETUS

Tasmacetus shepherdi
Sheperd's beaked whale

ZIPHIUS

Ziphius cavirostris
Cuvier's beaked whale

DELPHINIDAE

CEPHALORHYNCHUS

Cephalorhynchus commersoni
Commerson's
dolphin

Cephalorhynchus eutropia
Black dolphin

Cephalorhynchus heavisidii
Heaviside's dolphin

Cephalorhynchus hectori
Hector's dolphin

DELPHINUS

Delphinus delphis

Common dolphin

Delphinus capensis
Delfino del capo

FERESA

Feresa attenuata
Pygmy killer whale

GLOBICEPHALA

Globicephala melas
Long-finned pilot whale

Globicephala macrorhynchus
Short-finned pilot whale

GRAMPUS

Grampus griseus
Risso's dolphin

LAGENODELPHIS

Lagenodelphis hosei
Fraser's dolphin

LAGENORHYNCHUS

Lagenorhynchus acutus
Atlantic white-sided
dolphin

Lagenorhynchus albirostris
White-beaked dolphin

Lagenorhynchus australis
White-beaked dolphin

Lagenorhynchus cruciger
Hourglass dolphin

Lagenorhynchus obliquidens
Pacific white-sided
dolphin

Lagenorhynchus obscurus
Dusky dolphin

LISSODELPHIS

Lissodelphis borealis
Northern rightwhale dolphin

Lissodelphis peroni
Southern rightwhale dolphin

ORCINUS

Orcinus orca
Killer whale

PEPONOCEPHALA

Peponocephala electra
Melon-headed whale

PSEUDORCA

Pseudorca crassidens
False killer whale

SOUSA

Sousa chinensis
Indo-Pacific hump-backed dolphin

Sousa teuszii
Atlantic hump-backed dolphin

SOTALIA

Sotalia fluviatilis
Tucuxi

STENELLA

Stenella attenuata
Pantropical spotted
dolphin

Stenella clymene
Clmymene dolphin

Stenella coeruleoalba
Striped dolphin

Stenella frontalis
Atlantic spotted dolphin

Stenella longirostris
Long-snouted spinner
dolphin

STENO

Steno bredanensis
Rough-toothed dolphin

TURSIOPS

Tursiops truncatus
Bottlenose dolphin

PHOCOENIDAE

AUSTRALOPHOCAENA

Australophocaena dioptrica
Spectacled porpoise

NEOPHOCAENA

Neophocaena phocaenoides
Finless porpoise

PHOCOENA

Phocoena phocoena
Harbour porpoise

Phocoena sinus
Vaquita

Phocoena spinipinnis
Burmeister's porpoise

PHOCOENOIDES

Phocoenoides dalli Dall's
porpoise

A

B

C

Table - Systems analysis is a science in progress, ever subject to revision or new discoveries. This is particularly true in the case of the cetaceans as although they arouse great public interest we actually know very little about them. Moreover, it is still possible that new species will be discovered - during the preparation of this book we learnt of the discovery of a new species of beaked whale, the Mesoplodon bahamondi. The classification presented here therefore includes the most up-to-date information and readers maybe find differences compared with those published elsewhere.

A, B, C, D - The order of the cetaceans is divided into two suborders: Mysticetes or cetaceans with baleen like the humpback whale (A) and the Odontocetes or whales with teeth like the white whale (D). The suborders are divided into large families. There is an ample discussion in course in the scientific community about the systematic arrangement of entire families or simply of some species. The most controversy cases refer to the sperm whale (B) which, according to some, could be a whale even though provided with teeth, and the bottlenose dolphins from which there exist various species instead of only one, the Bottlenose dolphin (C), as retained by many.

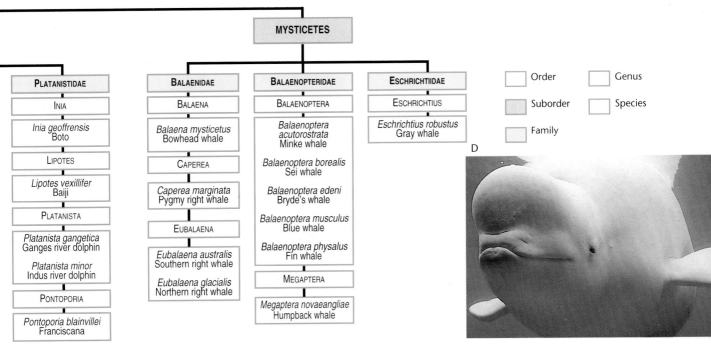

MYSTICETES _(Suborder)_

PLATANISTIDAE _(Family)_
- **INIA** _(Genus)_
  - *Inia geoffrensis* — Boto
- **LIPOTES**
  - *Lipotes vexillifer* — Baiji
- **PLATANISTA**
  - *Platanista gangetica* — Ganges river dolphin
  - *Platanista minor* — Indus river dolphin
- **PONTOPORIA**
  - *Pontoporia blainvillei* — Franciscana

BALAENIDAE
- **BALAENA**
  - *Balaena mysticetus* — Bowhead whale
- **CAPEREA**
  - *Caperea marginata* — Pygmy right whale
- **EUBALAENA**
  - *Eubalaena australis* — Southern right whale
  - *Eubalaena glacialis* — Northern right whale

BALAENOPTERIDAE
- **BALAENOPTERA**
  - *Balaenoptera acutorostrata* — Minke whale
  - *Balaenoptera borealis* — Sei whale
  - *Balaenoptera edeni* — Bryde's whale
  - *Balaenoptera musculus* — Blue whale
  - *Balaenoptera physalus* — Fin whale
- **MEGAPTERA**
  - *Megaptera novaeangliae* — Humpback whale

ESCHRICHTIIDAE
- **ESCHRICHTIUS**
  - *Eschrichtius robustus* — Gray whale

Legend: Order, Suborder, Family, Genus, Species

D

To complicate the picture of monophyletic theory, there are various interpretations of the similarities among various species.

The most emblematic case is the sperm whale. Recently Milinkovoch (1995) analyzed a portion of the DNA sequence and cytochrome *b* of the mitochrondria of the sperm whale gene, finding a similarity between the sperm whale family (including dwarf and pygmy sperm whales), which are odontocetes, and the rorqual family, which are mysticetes. His investigation comes to the conclusion that, although sperm whales have teeth, they are phylogenetically closer to baleen whales than to other odontocetes, and asserts that the common progenitor could have lived 10-15 million years ago. Nevertheless, this hypothesis does not take into consideration other families of mysticetes such as right whales and gray whales.

Heyning, on the contrary, holds that sperm whales should remain in the Odontocetes suborder, and to support his theory, he has compared 75 morphological features of all families of cetaceans in existence and all fossil remains so far discovered. In addition, it should be noted that there are fossil remains of ancient physeterids from 25-30 million years ago, which conflicts with the hypothesis of a common progenitor for rorquals and sperm whales.

There are even more problems in studying the systematics of cetaceans. According to some, the number of living species is much higher than the 81 now recognized. Factors like individual variability in colour, skeletal characteristics, the presence of subpopulations, and interfecundity with animals from species deemed different all add to this uncertainty.

The most well-known cases involve the bottlenose dolphin, the pilot whale and the common dolphin. Thus, both popular and scientific works abound with classifications based on one or another interpretation. Diversity can be found not only at the species level, but even in genus and family. Sometimes there is confusion even on how to write the name of a species.

The International Code of Nomenclature is based on the use of Latin as a scientific language, and establishes rules for transforming and attributing names. One of these rules advises not to use the double "i" in forming the genitive derived from proper names of persons or places. We have followed this recommendation here. For example, in other volumes the scientific name of the Commerson's dolphin, named after the French botanist and naturalist who first described this species, is written as *Cephalorhynchus commersonii*, while we always use *Cephalorhynchus commersoni*. On the contrary, *Cephalorhynchus heavisidii*, named after Commander Heaviside,

captain of the ship that brought the first specimen to London, is correct due to the Latin transformation of the name to Heavisidius.

To facilitate reading scientific names, it is important to note that when the Latin name of the species is accompanied by a proper name and a date, this indicates the scientist who first described it and the year of the first publication. If the scientific name of the species has been changed in later revisions, the name of the scientist and the year are still included, but are noted within parentheses.

There are 34 genera in the Odontocetes suborder. They live in all the oceans and seas of the world, and some species have colonized large rivers. The male is often larger than the female, they have a very complex social life, and they all have teeth. Although they have teeth due to the fact that they are predators, the surrounding environment and availability of resources have changed and adapted them, so that the teeth of some species have been reduced to an insignificant number and are no longer functional.

Members of the Mysticetes suborder are larger, the female is generally bigger than the male, and they are great migrators who move between the Poles and the Equator, depending on the season. They all have baleen, but the number, density and length varies from species to species.

A MAMMAL THAT LIVES LIKE A FISH

The cetacean body is designed to provide the least hydrodynamic resistance while swimming, with skin that also has some special features that increase the efficiency of the caudal fin's propulsive thrust. Externally, cetaceans are similar to fish, especially the great pelagic swimmers, due to their extremely tapered body, colour, and the presence of fins. The powerfully muscular flukes are compressed laterally to offer less resistance to the water and provide greater support for the caudal fin, which is horizontal, the only external difference from fish. For this reason, cetaceans swim by moving the back portion of the body dorsoventrally. The flukes are so powerful that an animal weighing over 50 tons can make spectacular leaps out of the water.

Some dolphin species are extremely fast swimmers and can travel over 50 km an hour, while others like beaked whales can remain underwater for long periods of time, and sperm whales can dive to depths of 3,000 m.

While odontocetes are not as big as mysticetes, they can nevertheless become quite large. This increase in size seems to be a response to the problem of heat loss. Proportionally speaking, larger animals have a smaller body surface and thus less dispersion of heat. Not only does the form of these animals make them particularly adapted to living in the water, but their skin and fins also play a fundamental role in making them perfectly hydrodynamic.

Living in water has also modified their physiology, which has adopted all the most efficient solutions.

A - Cetaceans are mammals which have returned to the sea or ocean; they have adopted the exterior semblance of fish and have modified both their metabolism and some physiological functions in order to better adapt to the medium in which they live. They have kept all the distinctive aspects of mammals such as breathing with the lungs, nursing the young and forging complex social relationships. Cetaceans jump for different reasons and it is common in both odontocetes and mysticetes like these two humpback whales.

It can represent a social manifestation, a show of strength, a ritual flight during a mating contest, a game played by mothers with their young, a need to produce sounds or, more simply, the need for a little physical exercise.

B - Cetaceans are uncommonly social animals; dolphins of the spotted dolphin genus are among the most gregarious species. They swim together, seemingly in a random way, but in practice the school has a well defined structure in which each animal has its place depending on age and sex.

C - Unlike other mammals, cetaceans, which have adapted to long periods in apnoea, can reach great depths without encountering problems of embolism.
The ductile rib cage can resist high pressures.
The undisputed diving champion is the sperm whale which can reach depths of 3,000 m.

C

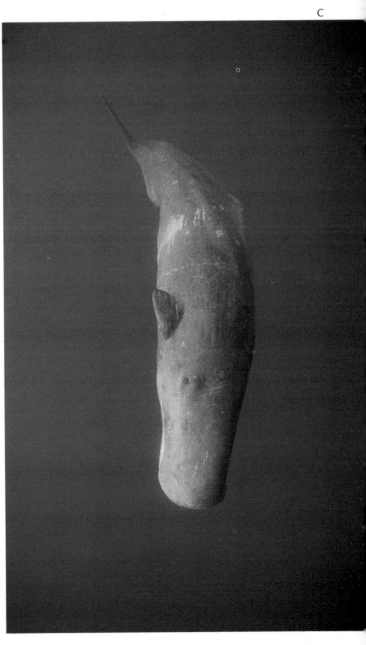

A

C

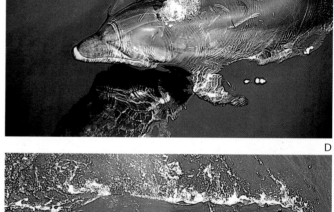

D

A - Apparently smooth, the dolphin's skin is covered in many microfolds which improve the efficiency of the swimming, avoiding phenomena of turbulence.

If you stroke a dolphin, its skin feels smooth and soft, yet its entire surface is covered by microfolds which direct the flow of water and avoid turbulence while swimming quickly. Thus, its skin is a complex organ capable of changing in order to optimize movement in water.

Its skin is an average of 2-4 mm thick, 10-20 times thicker than a land mammal's, and a beluga's skin may be as much as 12 mm thick. The dermal layer contains various

B

B - The "holes" which cetaceans have on their head are called "blowholes" and correspond to our nostrils. In all odontocetes, such as the sperm whale, the nostrils open into a single blowhole. In the case of this large cetacean the opening is in an asymmetric position on the left side of the head; this is the result of a special adaptation to diving to great depths.

receptors with multiple functions, many of which are not yet completely understood. The tactile receptors are distributed over the entire body surface, but the most sensitive areas are near the head, the pectoral fins, the naval and the genital area. As they evolved, cetaceans lost their fur, but some species have retained their vibrissae, which have a tactile function, like a cat's whiskers. They are completely absent in the narwhal and the beluga, while they are present only in the embryo of the pilot whale and the dolphin, in newborn bottlenose dolphins, rough-toothed dolphins and members of the Stenella genus, and in the adults of several species of whales, the river dolphin and the boto. There are areas around the blowhole which are particularly sensitive to changes in pressure, making it possible to open and close the hole while emerging and diving.

Special sacs enclose the mammary glands and genital organs, which can be everted when necessary.

The subcutaneous layer of fat, which is generally quite thick, helps avoid the dispersion of heat, makes the body more rounded and balances the animal's weight, making it easier to float. Even the skin colour is an adaptation to life in the sea. A uniform colour means that the animal does not need to camouflage itself, an indication that it is either quite large and has no enemies, or else hunts in deep waters at night. The sperm whale is typical of this category. Cetaceans living in oceanic waters have a dark dorsal area and a white ventral area. This has a mimetic function which is used by pelagic fish as well; seen from above, they blend into the deep blue depths, while seen from below they look like a reflection of the water's surface. This mimicry is effective both against predators and prey, and is common in dolphins.

The killer whale, which uses hunting techniques based on its high visibility, has developed contrasting patches on its skin. The black dolphin, which imitates the killer whale's colouring, does so for protective purposes. Its flukes and head are black, broken by a large white patch, and this confuses an attacking predator, reducing fatal attacks by 50%. The stripes along the body, characteristic of many members of the dolphin family, make the animal's contours vaguer and perform the same protective function. The white spots on the Atlantic spotted dolphin also mimic the reflections of the sun on the water. The alternating light spots and dark streaks around the mouth act to disorient prey, which cannot tell when the mouth is open. The white spots around the mouth of the sperm whale act like a mirror, reflecting luminescent prey and attracting it, while bioluminescent bacteria may also adhere near the mouth, making it luminous as well.

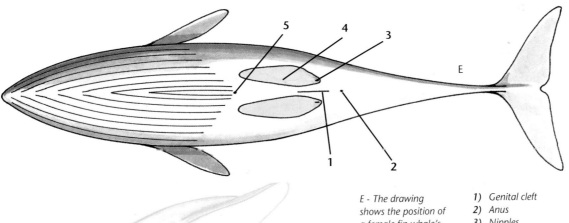

E - The drawing shows the position of a female fin whale's mammary glands. Each nipple is internally protected by a pocket which opens up on the sides of the genital cleft.

1) Genital cleft
2) Anus
3) Nipples
4) Mammary glands
5) Umbilicus

F - A cetacean's milk is thicker than that of terrestrial animals; it has just 40% to 55% of water but it is richer in fats (30%-40%) and proteins (75-20%). Just one year after its birth the young bottlenose dolphin in the photograph, now weaned, will be almost the same size as its mother.

C - In the photo a bottlenose dolphin is surfacing to breathe. Cetaceans begin to exhale before they reach the surface so as to begin inhaling in the short period, just three seconds, the head remains above the water. It is also interesting to note that the blowholes are abundantly innervated by nerve endings and have numerous mechanoreceptors which allow the blowhole to open and close as they surface and dive.

D - The whale and fin whale's nostrils open into two separate blowholes which can be seen clearly in this photo of a humpback whale surfacing.

A

A - The long-finned pilot whale is a medium-dimensioned cetacean which reaches 7 m in length; its body is black with a large dorsal gray area and an elongated white ventral spot.

B - The sperm whale feeds in the ocean depths and mainly on luminous prey. This luminescence is produced by bacteria which can remain around the mouth after feeding, close to the clearly visible white marks also in the specimen photographed. These marks reflect the light of the bacteria and attract the prey.

B

C

D

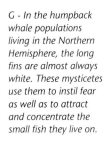

E, H - The photographs show two dusky dolphins (E) and a couple of Pacific white sided dolphins (H). The reflection of the rays through the surface of the sea is perfectly imitated by the marks and shading on their bodies, which deceive predators from below. This effect is accentuated by the fact that these animals live in schools and often swim close to each other.

F, I - The Pantropical spotted dolphin (F) and the Atlantic spotted dolphin (I) are species which live in the high seas and have small white and black spots which mimic the reflection of the sun on the water while the dark coloured back and white belly help to camouflage the animal from respectively above and below.

G - In the humpback whale populations living in the Northern Hemisphere, the long fins are almost always white. These mysticetes use them to instil fear as well as to attract and concentrate the small fish they live on.

On the contrary, in the populations of the Southern Hemisphere, the fins are darker because the chief prey are small crustaceans so the hunting technique is different.

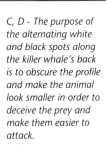

C, D - The purpose of the alternating white and black spots along the killer whale's back is to obscure the profile and make the animal look smaller in order to deceive the prey and make them easier to attack.

J - The young Atlantic spotted dolphins have different colouring to that of the adults. They do not have the numerous white spots of the adult animals.

THE FINS

A

B

C

D

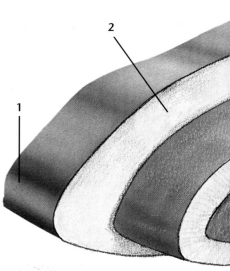

1

2

E

F

by cooling the blood. This takes place through the fins, which have no fatty layer and are abundantly supplied with blood vessels, thus functioning as heat exchangers.

The shape of dorsal fins may vary from species to species and individual to individual. There are at least three types: the falcate dorsal fin, as in dolphins, the triangular fin, as in male killer whales, and the rounded fin, as in the Hector's dolphin. Some species have none, such as the narwhal, the finless porpoise and the rightwhale dolphin. The caudal fin in almost all odontocetes is falcate and divided into two symmetrical flukes, with the back edge separated by an incisure down the middle. In beaked whales, this incisure is absent or reduced. Markings, form, colour and size of the flukes are not only characteristic of the species, but also of each individual. They provide useful information in scientific research based on photoidentification, especially in migration studies.

Cetaceans have three types of fins, which, as in fish, serve to propel and direct the animal. The pectoral fins and the dorsal fin direct and stabilize movements, while the caudal fin gives impulse to the movement. Only the front limbs and pectoral girdle of their four-legged ancestors remain, with a skeletal structure consisting of a scapula, humerus, radius, ulna, carpus, metacarpus, and phalanxes. The back legs are absent, with vestiges (pelvic rudiments) remaining to which the muscles that support the male reproductive apparatus are connected. The dorsal and caudal fins have no skeleton; their rigidity is due to a connective tissue densely traversed by interwoven fibers.

Thermal insulation, provided by subcutaneous fat, is so efficient that body temperature needs to be regulated

A, B - The pectoral fins also help the animal swim in the desired direction and they correspond to our arms. Each species have differently shaped pectoral fins. Killer whales have rounded fins (A) which can reach lengths of 5 metres while humpback whales (B) have flexible pectoral fins.

C, D, E, F - The dorsal fins have no skeleton and act as stabilisers. In some species they are absent, in others they represent distinct characteristics and are in close relationship with the type of life that the cetaceans conduct and with the environment in which they live. The pictures show the fins of a dolphin (C), of a killer whale (D), of a Hector's dolphin (E) and of a long-finned pilot whale (F).

Drawing - When cetaceans are overheated their blood pressure increases and activates a peripheral circulation at the fins and for this reason these are abundantly supplied. The cross-section of a pectoral fin shows the presence of a network of veins wrapped around the arteries: heat is expelled because the arteries, expanding, transmit the heat of the blood to the outer veins and these in turn expel it into the water.

1) Cutaneous layer
2) Subcutaneous layer
3) Veins
4) Ulna
5) Arteries
6) Radius

H

I

J

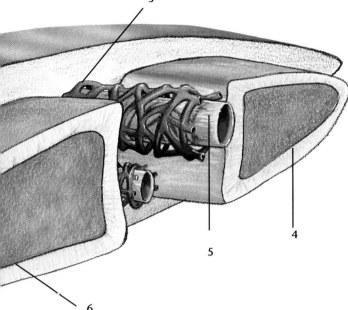

G

G, I - The dolphin family's tail fins are designed for high speed swimming and allow more rapid movement than those of the mysticetes. The images show the tail fins of three spotted dolphins (G) and of a long-finned pilot whale (I).

H, J - Tail fins have no skeleton nor subcutaneous fat; they are supported by an extremely rigid muscular material. Unlike fish fins, they are positioned horizontally and so the thrust needed to swim is provided from the top down and vice versa. The tail fins of whales and blue whales can be up to 6 m wide, up to 4 m wide in the case of the humpback whale (H) and 3.5 metres in the case of the sperm whale (J).

45

THE SIGHT

Cetaceans have eyes similar to those of ungulates.

The curvature of the lens can be changed in order to focus, permitting the animal to see clearly both in and out of the water. This ability is amplified by the special structure of the pupil, which has an elliptical form that may have two holes, used in different situations. The eye is also sensitive to minimum quantities of light, as demonstrated by the fact that bioluminescent prey has been found in the stomachs of many species.

Cetaceans who live in rivers have had to adapt to low illumination and murky waters. Their vision is no longer functional and is replaced by the sense of touch. Indeed, they swim on their sides so that they can touch the bottom with the pectoral fin. They also have highly developed biosonar which they use continuously to "see" what is happening around them.

A

B

Drawing D
1) *Larynx*
2) *Palate-pharyngal muscles*
3) *Upper jaw bone*

D

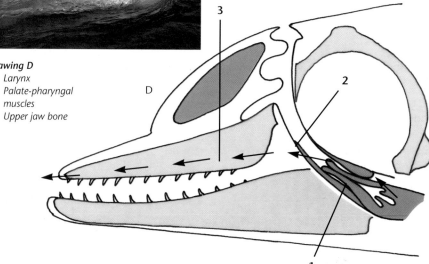

3

2

1

THE HEARING

To reduce friction in the water, cetaceans have no pinnae, and the external ear is thus reduced to a small hole. It appears that sounds are received through the thin mandibular bones and transmitted to the inner ear through the fatty material that surrounds the tympanic bone.

When humans are completely underwater, sounds seem to arrive from all directions, making it

C

A, B, C - Cetaceans have good eyesight both in and out the water thanks to powerful muscles which allow them to rapidly adapt their dioptric system and to the particular shape of the pupil. When resting, their eyes can see things up close;

even when the water is clear their visibility in this state rarely exceeds 50 m and it would be pointless to try to see any further. In the images, from top to bottom, a bottlenose dolphin, a white whale, and a right whale are shown.

D, E - The mechanisms used by odontocetes to emit the characteristic sounds have still not been fully understood. There are two more widely upheld theories. In the first the larynx is considered to be the point at which the sound is created by the vibrations of the

epiglottis cartilage (D 1); the sound, transmitted to the snout by the palatopharyngeal (D 2) muscles is directed outwards by the bones of the upper jaw (D 3) and the sounds are received by the ears through the outer auditory passage. The second theory, more credited, suggests that the vibration of the walls of the tabular sac (E 1) of the nostrils (E 2) produce sounds which, reflected by the frontal cranium bones (E 3) and by the upper jaw bones, pass through the adipose structure of the melon (E 4) which acts as an acoustic lens, concentrating them and directing them outwards. Sound is received through the lower jaw which transmits it to the tympanic bulla (E 5) and then to the inside ear.

impossible to determine their exact origin. Cetaceans cannot afford this approximation, and their ears are modified in ways which avoid this problem. The tympanic bone is insulated from the rest of the cranial bone by fatty material, and within it the sensitive part of the ear is insulated by a capsule containing air. Changes in density of all these structures help identify the origin of sounds.

The number of cells that innervate the ear (two or three times as many as in humans) and the larger auditory nerve suggest an excellent capacity to distinguish tones and high frequency sound waves.

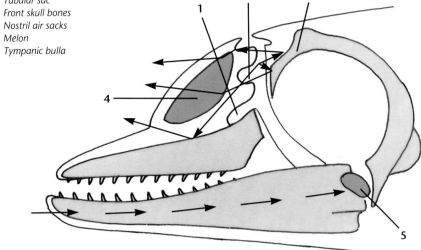

Drawing E
1) Tabular sac
2) Front skull bones
3) Nostril air sacks
4) Melon
5) Tympanic bulla

THE ECHOLOCATION

Adaptation to an environment in which visibility is significantly reduced, under the best of circumstances to only a few dozen meters, has not limited the visual ability of cetaceans, but has led them to develop a sophisticated system of sound production and reception for echolocation.

Sound travels through the air at about 340 m a second, while in water its speed is nearly five times faster. For this reason, acoustic communication plays a fundamental role in the water. Like other marine organisms, for example the invertebrates and fish, cetaceans are capable of producing a great variety of sounds useful for communicating among themselves, obtaining information on the surrounding environment, navigating and feeding. A system of echolocation, or biosonar, is typical of odondocetes, but even the mysticetes seem capable of utilizing this system of acoustic "vision." The sounds emitted for echolocation are generally very high frequency, over 200,000 cycles a second.

The penetration of sound waves is inversely proportional to frequency, and cetaceans modulate it as necessary. During normal swimming conditions, low frequency sounds are emitted, with a range of action of a few dozen km. The frequency changes once the return echo identifies something that arouses interest, and when the objective is close by, high frequency sounds can be used to obtain more detailed information.

THE LANGUAGE

Numerous studies on animals in captivity and in the wild have shown that these marine mammals are capable of communicating with each other using "language." Although it cannot be compared to human language, it is nevertheless an articulate system of communication, in which sounds are modulated in tone and frequency and are repeated constantly during specific actions and particular situations. Dialects typical of groups of individuals have been identified within populations of the same species, as in the case of killer whales living along the coast of British Columbia. Mother and calf recognize each other through sounds defined as "signature whistles," which note the difference from one individual to another, as occurs in the human voice.

Special studies have shown that belugas use these recognition signals to communicate and coordinate group hunts. It is thus probable that other species of cetaceans use the same methods to regulate synchronous movements of the hundreds of individuals that make up a herd.

The ability to utilize sounds is not limited to this; it appears that some species, like the bottlenose dolphin, are capable of producing booms of over 230 decibels. Known as sprays, they are lethal to fish and are used as a hunting weapon.

ECHOLOCATION

Species	Frequency (kHz)	Duration (μs)	Watching conditions
Commerson's dolphin	120-134	180-600	captivity
Hector's dolphin	112-130	140	open sea
White whale	100-115	50-60	bay
Common dolphin	23-67	50-150	open sea
Pilot whale	50-60	-	captivity
Risso's dolphin	65	40-100	bay
Boto	95-105	200-250	river
Pacific white-sided dolphin	30-60	-	captivity
Baiji	100-120	-	captivity
Narwhal	40	250	open sea
Finless porpoise	128	127	captivity
Irrawaddy dolphin	50-60	150-170	captivity
Killer whale	14-20	210	captivity
Harbour porpoise	120-140	130-260	captivity
Dall's porpoise	120-160	180-400	open sea
River dolphin	15-60	-	captivity
False killer whale	100-130	100-120	bay
Rough-toothed dolphin	5-32	-	captivity
Tucuxi	95-100	120-200	river
Bottlenose dolphin	110-120	50-80	bay

Table - The characteristics of the biosonar signals of different species of odontocetes indicate that, with few exceptions, the sounds emitted are at high frequency - between 30 and 160 chilohertz (kHz) - and very short. In the reported cases the maximum is 6,000 microseconds (μs) in the dolphin.

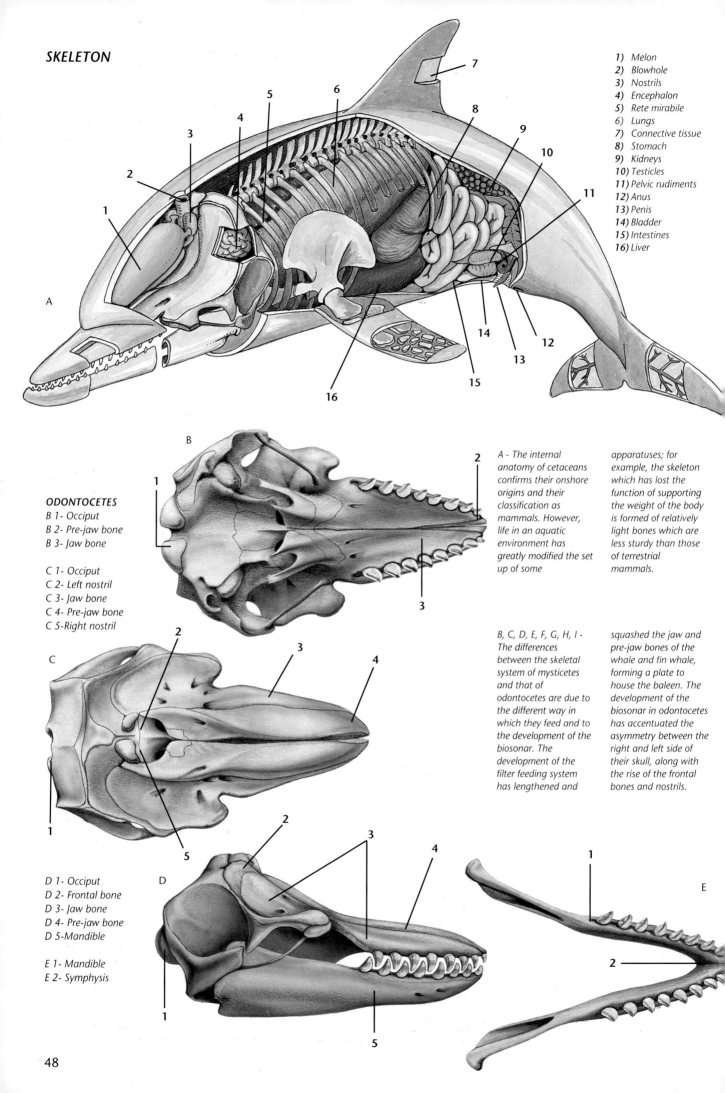

SKELETON

1) Melon
2) Blowhole
3) Nostrils
4) Encephalon
5) Rete mirabile
6) Lungs
7) Connective tissue
8) Stomach
9) Kidneys
10) Testicles
11) Pelvic rudiments
12) Anus
13) Penis
14) Bladder
15) Intestines
16) Liver

ODONTOCETES

B 1- Occiput
B 2- Pre-jaw bone
B 3- Jaw bone

C 1- Occiput
C 2- Left nostril
C 3- Jaw bone
C 4- Pre-jaw bone
C 5-Right nostril

D 1- Occiput
D 2- Frontal bone
D 3- Jaw bone
D 4- Pre-jaw bone
D 5-Mandible

E 1- Mandible
E 2- Symphysis

A - The internal anatomy of cetaceans confirms their onshore origins and their classification as mammals. However, life in an aquatic environment has greatly modified the set up of some apparatuses; for example, the skeleton which has lost the function of supporting the weight of the body is formed of relatively light bones which are less sturdy than those of terrestrial mammals.

B, C, D, E, F, G, H, I - The differences between the skeletal system of mysticetes and that of odontocetes are due to the different way in which they feed and to the development of the biosonar. The development of the filter feeding system has lengthened and squashed the jaw and pre-jaw bones of the whale and fin whale, forming a plate to house the baleen. The development of the biosonar in odontocetes has accentuated the asymmetry between the right and left side of their skull, along with the rise of the frontal bones and nostrils.

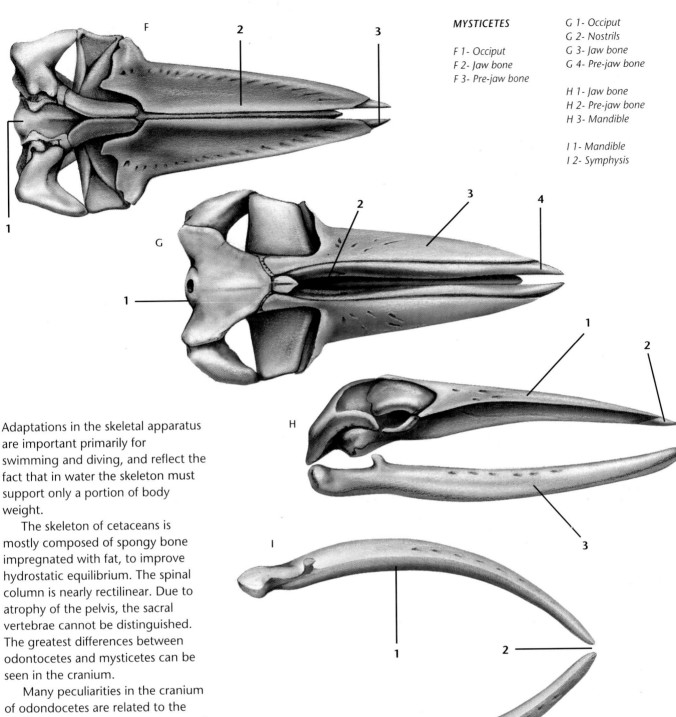

Adaptations in the skeletal apparatus are important primarily for swimming and diving, and reflect the fact that in water the skeleton must support only a portion of body weight.

The skeleton of cetaceans is mostly composed of spongy bone impregnated with fat, to improve hydrostatic equilibrium. The spinal column is nearly rectilinear. Due to atrophy of the pelvis, the sacral vertebrae cannot be distinguished. The greatest differences between odontocetes and mysticetes can be seen in the cranium.

Many peculiarities in the cranium of odondocetes are related to the presence of special organs associated with sound production and reception and diving. The premaxillar and maxillar bones are elongated to the front and to the back, extending over the orbital region. In addition, there is a strong asymmetry between the right and the left sides, due to the development of a fatty organ known as the melon.

In mysticetes, the modifications in the cranium can be traced to their particular feeding specialization and the development of baleen. The maxillar and premaxillar bones are elongated only to the front.

In rorquals, the supraoccipital bone covers the frontal bones.

SKELETON SYSTEM	ODONTOCETES (B, C, D, E)	MYSTICETES (F, G, H, I)
Temporal and palatine vomer	Not much developed	Well developed
Cranium symmetry	Asymmetrical	Symmetrical
Pterygoid bone	Complex	Flat
Choane margins or posterior spout holes	Formed by the pterygoid bone	Formed by the palatine bones
Occiput condyles	Turned on the back	Turned on the dorsal side
Teeth or baleen plates in the embryo	Teeth	Teeth
Teeth or baleen plates in the adult	Teeth	Baleen plates
Well developed mandible symphysis	Yes	No
Mouth closing	Complete	Incomplete
Mandible concavity	Towards the outside	Towards the inside
Hyoid bone	With mobile articulation	Without articulation
Sternum composition	Several bones	A single bone
Segments between ribs and sternum	Present	Absent
Number of ribs articulated with sternum	A minimum of 3 ribs	Only the first pair
Thorax	Mobile	Rigid
Pelvic bones	Columnar	Triangular
Number of digits	4	4 (5 in Balæna)

THE BRAIN

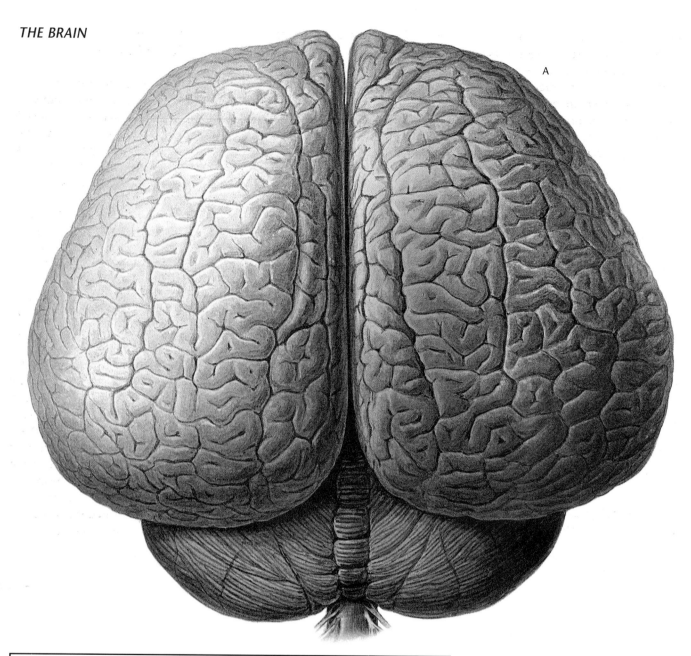

A

ENCEPHALISATION

Species	encephalon weight (g)	body weight (kg)	lenght (cm)	encephalisation quotient
Bottlenose dolphin	1632	116	226	0,0141
Dolphin	1125	91	185	0,0124
Striped dolphin*	207	4	68	0,0575
Tucuxi	688	42	158	0,0163
White whale	1505	340	305	0,0044
Narwhal*	1370	83	185	0,0166
Pilot whale	2475	258	269	0,0104
Killer whale	6050	495	549	0,0122
Sperm whale	9200	36700	1494	0,0003
Humpback whale	7500	29749	1372	0,0003
Fin whale	5000	40823	1920	0,0001
Sei whale	4900	22680	1585	0,0002

*New born individuals

The cetacean brain is globular in form, probably due to an anteroposterior compression of the cranium caused by changes in form during evolution. The cerebral hemispheres almost completely cover the cerebellum and have more convolutions than in other mammals.

According to some researchers, these convolutions, similar to those in humans, indicate high intelligence, while others believe that the increased complexity of the brain is simply a consequence of the increased volume. Comparing the size of the brain with the animal's body weight, we can see that the largest species have proportionally smaller brains. This is also true in relation to the growth of single individuals; younger animals have proportionally larger brains than adults. Some researchers believe that this phenomenon is a sign of lesser evolution. If this were true, the killer whale would be more evolved than the bottlenose dolphin. Others have observed that there is a correlation between the size of the brain and the duration of gestation (up to 16 months in the killer whale and 12 months in the bottlenose dolphin).

The encephalization coefficient, i.e. the relationship between the weight of the brain and body weight, can measure development and the ability to receive and process sensory stimulation by the cerebral cortex.

It is interesting to note that in dolphins, the encephalization coefficient is less than in humans, but well above that of other mammals, including primates.

The appearance of the cortex in terms of number of furrows, folds, depth, and variability, is comparable to humans and apes. Nevertheless,

details of the topography of sensory and motor areas reveal them to be more similar to those of carnivores.

Volume being equal, the brain surface area in some odontocetes is greater than that in humans. The increased surface area is due to a greater number of convolutions (in bottlenose dolphins it is 3,745 sq. cm, while in human it is 2,275 sq. cm). Nevertheless, in cetaceans the thickness of the cortex is an average 1.4 mm, thinner than in primates (2.9 mm in humans). Thus, its total volume is less: 560 cubic cm in the bottlenose dolphin compared with 660 in humans, but still more than a chimpanzee).

The cerebral hemispheres in odontocetes are clearly asymmetrical, like the cranium. In the bottlenose dolphin, the axis of sound emissions is deviated to the left, and it has been noted in captivity that they tend to swim in a counterclockwise direction, thus favouring the right hemisphere.

A HEART WITH A VARIABLE RHYTHM

The cetacean circulatory system is complex, and its functions are not yet fully understood. Cetaceans are capable of storing more oxygen in their muscles due to the action of a pigment known as myohemoglobin. The red corpuscles are larger and more numerous than in land mammals (0.0105 mm in diameter and from 7 to 11 million per cubic mm compared with 0.0075 mm in diameter and 5 million per cubic mm in humans). Blood weight varies from 5% to 9% of body weight.

The heart beats in various rhythms depending on the animal's activity. If it is on the surface, beats vary from 70 to 100 a minute, while underwater they drop to 30-40. But the structure most characteristic of the cetacean circulatory system is the *rete mirabile*, a network of capillaries located at various strategic points, in particular the brain and the thorax. Its function, among others, is to control changes in blood pressure when underwater. For this reason, the carotid artery does not carry blood directly to the brain, which is instead supplied through the dense *rete mirabile*.

Arterial system
Venous system
Rete mirabile

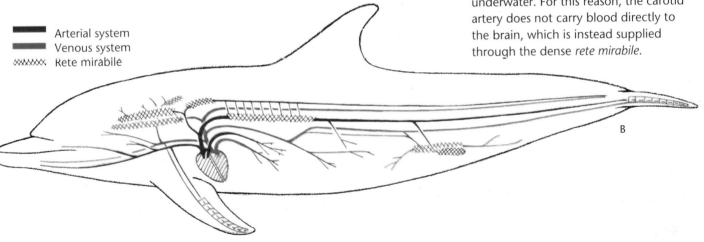

B

A - The cetacean's brain is as complex as that of the more evolved primates. The cerebral cortex has a larger surface than that of man thanks to the greater number of convolutions but its volume is smaller because it is thinner. The organisation of the sensorial and motive areas is similar to that of a terrestrial predator.

Table - The encephalisation quotient (EQ) is a value obtained dividing the weight of the encephalon of a given animal (EW) by the weight of its body (BW), in other words EQ=EW : BW.

B - The circulation of blood in cetaceans is characterised by the presence of numerous rete mirabile which are a tangle of capillaries whose functions are still not completely clear but which help to maintain the blood

pressure balanced and regulate the blood supply to important organs such as the brain. These nets are located in different parts of the body but the largest is positioned near the spinal column close to the thorax.

A RECORD-BREAKING APNEA

Cetaceans breathe by emerging with the dorsal tip of the cranium, where the nostrils open into the blowhole, which is formed by a single crack in odontocetes and two cracks in mysticetes. The lungs, like those of other marine mammals, are not lobed. All dimensions being equal, their volume is not significantly different from land mammals, but is proportionately smaller in species which reach profound depths. Cetaceans breathe less frequently than land mammals, and with each breath they can exchange 80% of the air inhaled. Thus, their lungs empty

deep dives, which is a problem in humans. The ability to cut off circulation to the ends of the large veins, maintaining supply only to the heart and brain, also helps avoid this problem. This, along with a slower heart rate (bradycardia) and the activation of anaerobic metabolism, saves and stores oxygen, making it possible to stay underwater for longer periods without breathing.

almost completely with each breath. Shortly before emerging, they exhale completely, and the overall act of breathing is extremely short, 0.3 seconds. Common dolphins, like bottlenoses, normally breath two or three times a minute, but after a long period underwater, frequency increases to 15-16 breaths.

The sperm whale dives deeper than any other cetacean (almost 3,000 m

deep for over 75 minutes).

Beaked whales can also reach notable depths, over 1,000 m, as can be deduced by the prey found in their stomachs. Special adaptations are necessary for this kind of performance in order to prevent embolisms and trauma caused by changes in pressure. The principal adaptations include a flexible ribcage, lungs and trachea full of elastic tissue, large, elastic veins, venous sinuses and a complex *rete mirabile* capable of containing a large amount of blood. Among other things, this has the function of filling spaces left empty by the compression of air. The *rete mirabile* and a different chemical composition of the blood, which is richer in heparin, seem to prevent the occurrence of aeroembolism after a long series of

A - Apnea performances depend greatly on feeding habits. Fin whales, in the photograph, and whales, feeding on epipelagic species, do not need to dive to great depths.

B - On the other hand, the bottlenose dolphin has coastal habits and prefers meso-pelagic and benthic-type fish which it seems to be able to catch at depths of more than 600 m.

C - Specimens which have become entangled in electric cables laid on the seabed have demonstrated that the

sperm whale can dive to depths of more than 2,500 m to catch the large bathyal cephalopods it loves.

D - Each type of cetacean, in relation to the behaviour of its prey, has developed different capabilities regarding the duration and the depth of immersion. The species which nourish themselves with coastal organisms do not exceed usually 200-300 m in depth, whereas those who nourish themselves with deep-sea fish must often look for food deeper than 1,000 m.

A RUMINANT'S STOMACH

Cetaceans have a stomach with a number of chambers, each of which has a different function, and like their ungulate progenitors, they use bacteria to digest food.

As we know, herbivorous mammals are not able to directly assimilate cellulose, the carbohydrate that constitutes plants. In ruminants like the ox, symbiotic bacteria in the first group of chambers in the stomach break it down into simpler substances which the animal can then utilize. The exoskeleton of crustaceans, the maxillae of

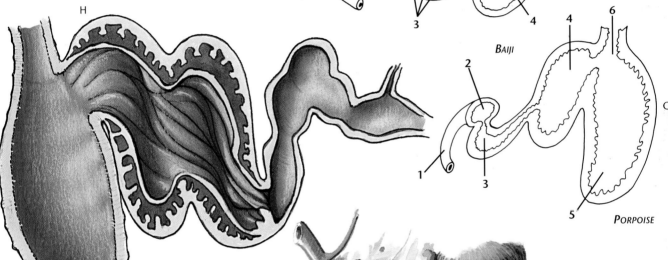

PLATANIST

BAIJI

PORPOISE

E, F, G - The division of the stomach into chambers varies from one species to another. For example, the front part of the platanist's stomach is formed by a pocket of the main chamber like that of the Ganges river dolphin (E) and the baiji (F) while the pyloric chamber is more complex than that of the porpoise (G).

1) Duodenum
2) Duodenal ampulla
3) Pyloric chamber
4) Main chamber
5) Front chamber
6) Oesophagus

cephalopods and parts of the bodies of other creatures cetaceans prey on are composed of chitin, a carbohydrate similar to cellulose. It is digested with the aid of bacteria similar to those present in the stomachs of ruminants.

In general, the cetacean stomach consists of a front chamber, a main chamber, a pyloric area and the duodenal ampulla. Nevertheless, the number of chambers can vary from species to species. In beaked whales, there may be as many as thirteen subdivisions, while the baiji and franciscana lack the first chamber.

The length of the intestine is also evidence of the cetacean kinship with ungulates; it varies from nine to over ten times the length of the body. It is less developed in odontocetes, with no caecum, while it is longer in mysticetes and the sperm whale.

H - The stomach of cetaceans is divided into chambers like that of ruminants to which they are closely related.

I - Living in an aquatic environment creates many osmoregulation problems for cetaceans because of the difference in the concentration of salt in the liquid in the animals' bodies and that of the sea water. To balance this osmotic difference cetaceans have exceptionally efficient kidneys made up of functional units called renunculi. These are actually small kidneys comprising a series of glomerules, loop of Henle and twisted distal tubules which have the function of saving the water and expelling the excess salt.

D

A

B

C

The taxonomic division of cetaceans into odontocetes and mysticetes also reflects their eating habits and the strategies they use to capture prey. The former are predators, while the latter are filter feeders.

Annelids, benthic crustaceans, shrimp, mollusks, squid, fish, reptiles, birds and mammals are all part of the broad diet of odontocetes. Based on their preferences, they can be divided into ichthyophagous species, which feed primarily on fish, teuthophagous species, which eat primarily cephalopods, and sarcophagous species, which eat not only fish, but also reptiles, birds and other species of cetaceans. Nevertheless, the availability of food plays a significant role in their choice of prey, and many cetaceans exhibit opportunistic behaviour. Thus, depending on the season or the geographical area, the same species may be either ichthyophagous or teuthophagous.

Odontocetes teeth cannot be used to chew, but to grasp and immobilize their prey. The form and the number of teeth are based on the various feeding specializations; dolphins have elongated jaws with numerous conical teeth, up to 300, which can be used to capture many types of prey, while porpoises have short jaws with teeth that resemble shovels; the flattened, rounded tip is useful for feeding on fish and invertebrates.

In primarily teuthophagous species, there are fewer teeth, and sometimes none at all. This is the case of the sperm whale and the grampus, which have teeth only on the lower jaw, or of the beaked whales, which may have no teeth at all.

A, D, E, F - The spotted dolphin (A) and the bottlenose dolphin (D, E, F,) possess numerous teeth, around 300 in total, set in both the upper and lower jaws. These teeth are conical and sharply pointed, characteristic of animals that have no particular alimentary preferences and adapt to the resources offered by their environment. In effect these cetaceans are capable of searching for food on the ocean bad but will also take pelagic prey.

E

F

B, C - The Atlantic white-sided dolphin belongs to the category of odontocetes with more teeth on the upper jaw than on the lower one. Normally they do not have more than 120 teeth and they prefer to feed on fish. The photograph shows a group of Atlantic white-sided dolphins attacking a shoal of small fish after having surrounded it with a clever hunting strategy.

A, D, E - The killer whale (D, E) and pseudo killer whale (A) have teeth on both jaws. In particular, the killer whale is a formidable hunter, its diet is varied and, along with the pseudo killer whale, it is the only cetacean which feeds on other mammals. In the waters of Patagonia it is possible to see male killer whales hunting eared seals right up to the beach (D) and then take the prey out to sea (E) where the female and young are waiting.

A

B

In these and the sperm whale, throat pleats are used to suck in and swallow prey whole, permitting them to expand the throat and create a depression that facilitates suction. Although it is not useful for feeding, the tooth of the male narwhal is the most remarkable of all: a single, characteristic elongated tooth that forms a spiral-shaped tusk.

Odontocetes use biosonar to locate prey, but they are also capable of producing extremely high frequency sounds to stun them. Some noises are also produced by violently slapping the tail on the water.

C

Odontocetes prey on creatures from a few centimetres to several metres in size, such as the large whales and rorquals which are sometimes attacked by groups of killer whales, the only true sarcophagous species.

Apart from these special cases, most odontocetes live on food chains with a high energy yield, using marine organisms which grow quickly and have a brief life span, so that a rapid renewal of the food resource will always provide them with a great quantity of nourishment.

C - The killer whale is a fearsome predator and has no particular alimentary preferences being able to adapt to all environments and the available resources. Even though the fish that inhabit the ocean floor are not its favourite food, this photo demonstrates that a ray has stimulated the appetite of a killer whale and has become easy prey.

D

E

B - The sperm whale has a lot of strong teeth on the lower jaw alone while on the upper jaw there are only small, useless, bent teeth.
The presence of teeth on the lower jaw alone or no teeth at all is typical of species which feed mainly or exclusively on cephalopods.

Daily consumption of food is proportionate to body weight and can vary from 3% to 14%, higher in the smaller odontocetes and lower in larger species. The caloric value of the prey also determines the quantity consumed. In general, fish and squid provide from 1 to 3 kilocalories per gramme.

Based on these values, it has been calculated that the entire population of sperm whales, about 2 million

individuals, eats at least 110 million tons of cephalopods a year.

In mysticetes, a filtering system made of baleen is used in place of teeth. These horny laminae are suspended from the upper jaws, and their number and length vary from species to species. The inner edge of each baleen is fringed and overlays the next one, forming a dense fibrous layer that constitutes the filtering structure.

Common whales have longer baleen, up to 5 m in length, while rorquals have shorter ones, no more than one m long in the blue whale. Due to their different feeding habits, the former have no baleen in the front of the jaw, as they feed by swimming slowly with their mouths open, while the latter do not have this diastema, are faster, and feed by collecting enormous quantities of water and food, which they filter by

pressing the tongue against the roof of the mouth.

Rorquals' system of feeding requires special anatomical structures. The presence of many throat pleats, which extend down to the belly, make it possible to dilate the mouth cavity to collect a greater amount of water and thus food. The weight of this volume is equal to a third of body weight, and it would be impossible for the rorqual to close its mouth without an elastic suspension of the jaw and the thrust of its own body. Thus, a blue whale weighing 150 tons can collect 50 tons of water mixed with food every time it opens its mouth.

A, B - Like all fin whales, the blue whale actively hunts for food and exploits the presence and concentration of shoals of pelagic prey. The throat pleats have the function of increasing the volume of the mouth to allow as much water and food as possible to enter.

A 150-ton blue fin whale can hold 50 cubic m of water in its mouth. To close its mouth it has to exploit the thrust of its weight assisting the action of the powerful muscles which support the lower jaw allowing the body to rotate laterally.

A

B

C

D

E

F

G

*E, G - After trapping
their prey in a turmoil
of bubbles emitted
from their blowholes,
the humpback whales
eat frenziedly, diving
on the terror-struck
small fish which are
unable to escape.*

*H - Krill is the favourite
food of the Antarctic
whale. The most
important species is the
Euphausia superba, a
small 6-cm long prawn.
It has been estimated
that the mysticetes
present in the Antarctic
consume more than 35
million tons of these
crustaceans every year.*

*C - Also the common
fin whale filters in an
active way. It has more
upper baleen than any
other species - up to
527 horny blades
along the perimeter of
the upper jaw. In the
Northern Hemisphere,
along with krill
(Meganictyphanes
norvegica), herring
(Clupea harengus) is
the main food of this
species.*

*D, F - Even if all the
animals seem to hunt
in the same way, each
species uses a different
system to concentrate
the prey available as
far as possible.
For example, the
humpback whale is the
mysticete which uses
most techniques; in
this case the animal
has attacked the prey,
swimming vertically to
the surface. The return
action makes it easier
to close its mouth and
expel the water.*

H

A - The gray whale is the only mysticetes which uses different hunting techniques unlike whales and rorquals which feed simply swimming with their mouths open, waiting for the food to be filtered by the baleen.

B - When migrating, the gray whale nibble the sprays of enormous algae called kelp, ingesting huge quantities.

C - The gray whale has around 160 baleen, fewer than all other mysticetes; these baleen are thick and short and are generally about half a metre long.

D - Gray whales migrate from the warm waters of Southern California to the colder ones of the Bering Sea. Even although the feeding grounds are located in the North, during migration these whales feed on a huge variety of organisms, hunting on the seabed and in open ocean.

Humpback whales use special hunting systems; they focus on schools of small fish, surrounding them in a net of bubbles, while the gray whales suck mud from the sea floor in search of small crustaceans. The quantity of food which mysticetes consume daily varies from 2% to 4% of body weight.

A blue whale is capable of eating 3 tons of shrimp a day.

The primary prey is crustaceans, including copepods, amphipods and euphausiids, or *krill*. Small pelagic fish like anchovies, sardines and herring are the most important prey in certain geographical areas and at certain times of the year.

Populations of the same species living in different hemispheres have different feeding habits. For example, the pygmy blue whale eats primarily crustaceans in the South, while in the North it prefers fish, especially gadiforms.

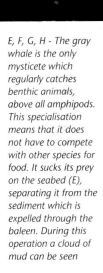

E

F

D

G

H

E, F, G, H - The gray whale is the only mysticete which regularly catches benthic animals, above all amphipods. This specialisation means that it does not have to compete with other species for food. It sucks its prey on the seabed (E), separating it from the sediment which is expelled through the baleen. During this operation a cloud of mud can be seen coming out of the whale's mouth (H). While feeding, it swims on its right side with its mouth close to the seabed, keeping its body at an angle of about 30° (F). This position is confirmed by the fact that the baleen on the right side of the mouth are worn down more than the others and by the fact that there are fewer ecto-parasites on the skin (acorn barnacles or canine teeth) because they have been detached by the abrasive action. The gray whale is also able to catch pelagic prey; some animals surround shoals of breeding squids or small fish, each whale in turn dives towards the prey with its mouth open and with a behaviour similar to the fin whale. This type of hunting is most common when the animals are migrating.

THE REPRODUCTION

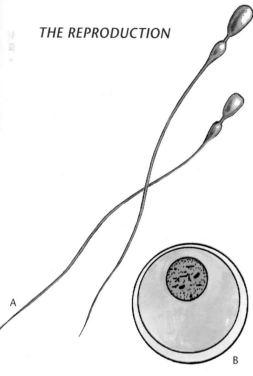

A - The sperm of cetaceans is similar to that of artiodactyles and shorter than human sperm. A humpback whale produces sperm which is 52.5 micron long, the sperm whale 40.6 micron while that of man is 55 micron long.

B - A cetacean's ovum is more or less the same size as that of a woman. Its diameter varies from 100 to 200 micron.

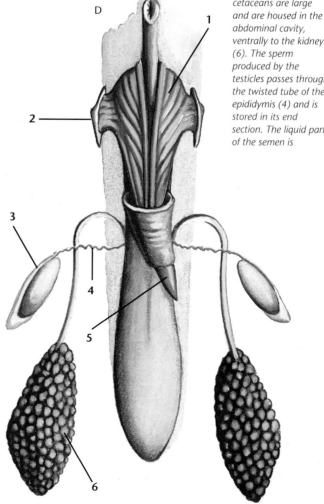

C - The penis measures about one tenth the length of the animal; in the larger animals it can reach a length of 3 m and have a diameter at the base of 30 cm.

At rest it is housed in a sac located halfway between the umbilicus and the anus and during erection two thirds of its length is released from the sac.

D - The testicles (3) of cetaceans are large and are housed in the abdominal cavity, ventrally to the kidneys (6). The sperm produced by the testicles passes through the twisted tube of the epididymis (4) and is stored in its end section. The liquid part of the semen is secreted by the prostate gland. The penis (5) is covered by a prepuce. During erection the penis is held in position by two retractor muscles (1). Inside the penis there are three columns made of fibrous tissue. Also the pelvic elements (2) play a role in the erection.

E - When they are swimming freely in the sea it is difficult to distinguish males from females, the only exception is the killer whale because the males are larger and have a high, triangular dorsal fin compared to the lower falciform one of the females and young animals.

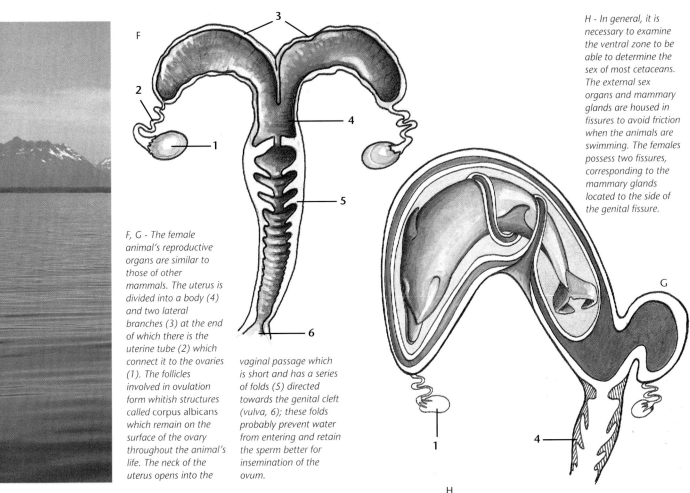

F, G - The female animal's reproductive organs are similar to those of other mammals. The uterus is divided into a body (4) and two lateral branches (3) at the end of which there is the uterine tube (2) which connect it to the ovaries (1). The follicles involved in ovulation form whitish structures called corpus albicans which remain on the surface of the ovary throughout the animal's life. The neck of the uterus opens into the vaginal passage which is short and has a series of folds (5) directed towards the genital cleft (vulva, 6); these folds probably prevent water from entering and retain the sperm better for insemination of the ovum.

H - In general, it is necessary to examine the ventral zone to be able to determine the sex of most cetaceans. The external sex organs and mammary glands are housed in fissures to avoid friction when the animals are swimming. The females possess two fissures, corresponding to the mammary glands located to the side of the genital fissure.

G

H

Reproductive behaviour is influenced by individual factors (age, degree of socialization, etc.) and by the environment (climate, geographical area, availability of food, etc.).

In general, mating is brief and may be preceded by complex courting rituals and competition among males, whose skin often bears the marks of battle. These struggles are never mortal, however, and in some species like the humpback whale, the female's choice is determined more by the male's singing ability than his physical strength.

Mating takes place in various ways. Depending on the species, the male and the female may mate vertically, stomach to stomach, or else they may position themselves next to each other, tilted side to side. In captivity, mating between different species has been observed, producing hybrids, and this may also occur under natural conditions.

It is possible to distinguish the two sexes externally in only a few species. In the killer whale, males have a very large, triangular dorsal fin that may be as much as 2 m high, while in females and younger individuals it is lower and falcate.

In some populations of the long-snouted spinner dolphin, males have a modified dorsal fin curved to the front, a dorsal hump and a swelling in the caudal region. Male narwhals have the characteristic tusk, resulting from the growth of one of the front teeth in the lower left jaw, while females normally do not have this tusk.

In all other cases, the ventral region must be examined in order to determine the sex of the animal. The sexual organs and mammary glands are enclosed in fissures to avoid damage while swimming.

Gestation varies and depends on the size of the animal. It may be as long as 16 months, as in the killer whale, or 8-11 months in the harbour

A

B

C

porpoise. Even the interval between two consecutive births may vary, from one to six years, and may be greatly influenced by outside circumstances. In their early stages, the embryos are very similar to those of other mammals. Rudimentary back legs, fingers and other structures are clearly evident in embryos 8 mm in size, although they disappear as the embryo develops. The fetus grows rapidly, and the ratio between the various body parts varies. As in other mammals, the cranium in the fetus and infants is proportionately larger than the rest of the body.

Calves are born with tails. Birth is generally quite brief, and the calf must immediately come to the surface to breathe, assisted by the mother. It is capable of following its mother by allowing itself to be carried in her

D

E

F

G

C, D - In the case of the misticeti, courting may be long and laborious while the actual act of mating is short with the animals joined abdomen to abdomen. The photographs show two right whales (C) and two killer whales (D).

E, F, H - The sequences show some stages in the courting habits of the Atlantic spotted dolphin: the animals delicately bite each other (E), in a sort of dance rub bodies and snouts (F), the male arouses the female by touching her genitalia (H).

G, I, J - Like the large cetaceans, also dolphins mate abdomen to abdomen for a very short period of time. The photographs show the spinner dolphin (I, J) and the Atlantic spotted dolphin (G).

A - Like all mammals, cetaceans are sociable animals and the fact that they reproduce by internal insemination implies a series of behavioural patterns and a life of social relations which range from the complex phases of courting to convince the female to mate, to competition among males as shown in this aerial photograph of a school of humpback whales.

B - This male grey whale clearly shows its intentions emerging with its penis everted and swimming on its back.

wake, keeping itself in a lateral-dorsal position without much effort. The calves nurse for over a year, even if they have already learned to eat alone. The weaning period depends on the mother's age, and is longer if she is near the end of her reproductive cycle. The mammary glands are in a ventral position near the genital fissure. The milk is generally richer in fats and more concentrated than human milk.

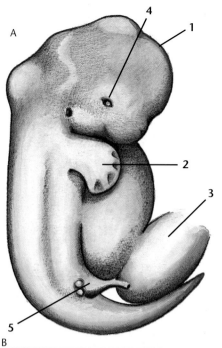

A

4

1

2

3

5

B

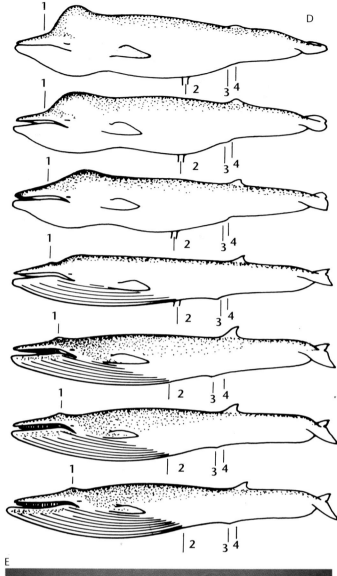

1   D

1   2   3 4

1   2   3 4

1   2   3 4

1   2   3 4

1   2   3 4

1   2   3 4

1   2   3 4

A - The early embryo of a cetacean is very similar to that of other mammals; there is no tail fin while elements and lower limbs can be noted.
1) Head
2) Front limbs
3) Umbilical cord
4) Eyes
5) Rudiments of the back limbs

B, E, F - New born mysticetes are between 1.6 m (pigmy right whale) and 7 m (blue fin whale) long. The newly born gray whale photographed in a bay of the Californian peninsula measures around 4.5 m (B). The young humpback whale swimming with its mother in the waters of Hawaii is no longer than 5 m (F) and the small white-skinned southern right whale was 5 m long at birth (E).

C

E

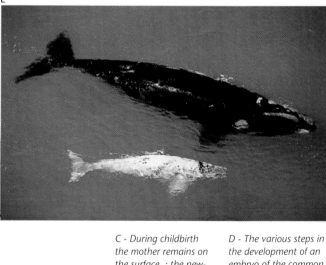

C - During childbirth the mother remains on the surface ; the new-born presents itself with the tail, unlike new-born of other mammals. When the baby is born the mother pushes it with its muzzle towards the surface so it can breathe.

D - The various steps in the development of an embryo of the common fin whale show the changing proportions between the various parts of the body and, in particular, of the size of the head.
1) Blowhole
2) Umbilicus
3) Genital cleft
4) Anus

G - The reproduction cycles of mysticetes are related to the maximum annual production of the prey on which they feed. Most whales and fin whales migrate long distances; after a period spent accumulating fat in the feeding grounds at the poles, they move to warm water to mate or give birth. When the young are weaned the return journey can begin. On average gestation lasts 12 months.

F

G

H

H - The reproductive behaviour of cetaceans is influenced by several factors such as season, socialisation, geographic and climatic situation. In odontocetes gestation is more variable than in mysticetes and depends on the size of the animal; on average it lasts 12 months while for the sperm whale it can last up to 15 months. In general females give birth to just one calf at a time and the interval between two births varies from one to six years depending on the number of animals in the population.

I, J - Although smaller, new born odontocetes are large animals. The young killer whale that is nursing measures around 2.5 metres (I) while the small long-finned pilot whale, swimming with its parents, (J) is little less than 1.5 m long.

I

J

LIFE IN SOCIETY

A - Even if the Risso's dolphin is a social animal, the formation of the group rarely supersedes a few tens of individuals.

Reproduction through internal fecundating and nursing the young are two fundamental reasons why mammals are social animals. The two individuals that mate require a complex series of behaviours in order to reduce aggression, and nursing creates a strong bond between mother and young that is the basis of the social system. There are different types of aggregations in cetaceans. Fresh water dolphins are mostly solitary and gather only for purposes of reproduction, while others, like the Atlantic white-sided dolphin, form schools of over a thousand individuals. Most aggregations of cetaceans lie somewhere between these two extremes.

This behaviour is no accident, but is rather the most effective adaptation for finding food, mating, raising young and defending themselves from predators in a unique environment like the sea.

The amount of cohesion and the size of the aggregation may change depending on the activity in which its members are engaged. When looking for food, pilot whales keep a certain distance from each other, covering a front a number of kilometres in size to expand the range of action. Once

B, C - The white whales move in groups and the subgroups of the group are formed of females accompanied by the off-spring and separated from the elder males. During the summer migration the elder males open the way (C). The group is concentrated at the mouth of the rivers which flow into the Arctic sea remaining in shallow water (B).

A

B

C

D

E

the prey has been located, they move together to hunt.

Cohesion between individuals is maintained through sight, sound and touch. Even the spectacular leaps of some species of dolphins may serve this purpose. The tail is often used to produce sounds and communicate with other individuals in the school. For example, if a ship comes too close, it may produce a reaction from one or more individuals, who will violently slap the surface of the water with their tails, perhaps as a gesture of intimidation.

D - The sperm whales live in aggregations formed of well-defined groups: the females live together with their off-spring of both sexes in groups of 20-40 individuals defined "mixed". The immature males gather together in aggregations which can even count up to 50 individuals. The elder males are usually secluded. During the mating season the groups get together for breeding.

E, G, H - The need for nourishment, the availability of space and food, the environment characteristics, the absence of predators and the fact to be mammals, rule the constitution of the group and the relationships between single individuals within the group itself. The groups can present different formations, some with fixed structures, others represent temporary aggregations for the immediate solution of a problem like hunting better or avoiding a danger. Striped (E), speckled (G) dolphins and the dolphins (H) can form groups of hundreds of individuals.

F - The signs on the body of these dolphins of the pygmy killer whale group have probably been caused by courting rituals or by competition between males of the same group.

H

Epimeletic behaviour, or helping another in difficulty, is common in many species of mysticetes and odontocetes. In bottlenose dolphins, individuals have been observed supporting a companion unable to swim, and often mothers will carry their dead calves on the surface for long periods of time, in a vain attempt to make them breathe.

A

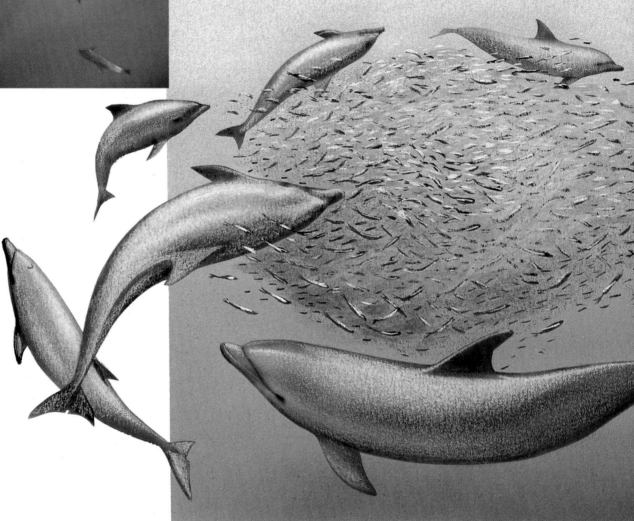

B

THREE DIFFERENT SOCIAL BEHAVIOURS

BOTTLENOSE DOLPHINS

Bottlenoses are probably the dolphins most commonly known to the public at large, because they are the cetaceans which best adapt to captivity; almost all dolphin aquariums in the world have examples of this species.

C

Thus, we know much more about its behaviour in captivity than in the wild. It is a gregarious animal that generally lives near the coast. It feeds mostly on fish, which it catches in shallow waters.

Bottlenose dolphins form schools that vary in size from two to several dozen animals. It has a complex social organization that includes the formation and disaggregation of groups. The primary groups are the most stable over time. Sometimes they will gather together for short periods, forming a single, larger secondary school that can hunt more

A, C, E, - The bottlenose dolphins form social groups formed from two to a few tens of individuals. The primary groups are composed of animals which remain together for some time; various primary groups can get together and form secondary groups. Such aggregations are less stable and are formed above all in deep water for obtaining better results in hunting (A, C). The primary groups are established on the basis of age and sex, the young males form groups defined as "bachelors", mothers and off-spring normally remain together for 3-6 years (E).

B - When the bottlenose dolphins find a shoal of deep-sea fish, they surround it and can use different techniques for hunting. Usually they perform a whirl around the prey, anti-clockwise, when they obtain a sufficient concentration of fish, they deep into this mass which resembles a boiling pot, where hundreds of prey are jumping agitated. The radius of this encirclement is in function to the size of the shoal and can vary between 25 and 150 m.

D

E

F

efficiently. Bottlenoses collaborate in this manner when they feed in the open sea in shallow waters.

When hunting, bottlenose dolphins organize and coordinate their actions according to systematic rules of behaviour. Russian researchers have observed the hunting techniques of bottlenoses in the Black Sea and have demonstrated the existence of a series of standard procedures. Searching for food may be the responsibility of the entire school or separate groups scattered throughout a vast area; individual

D, F - The search for food is usually carried out by the entire school (D), when they find the right type of fish, they surround them and use different tactics according to whether they are in shallow (F) or deep water. Sometimes a few individuals go hunting separately.

A

A, B, C, D, E, F, G - The repertoire of the leaps of the dolphins is extremely various. These joyful animals often come close to boats to profit from the wave caused by the engine (A, C), or simply they seem to show themselves off in acrobatic leaps as a game, in reality this behaviour may have a meaning and represent a form of communication (B, E, F, G).

B

C

D

E

F

animals scour small areas, moving randomly and frequently changing direction, speed and breathing rhythms.

Near the coast, the animals tend to close in on the prey and push it toward the coast, positioning themselves one next to another. If the prey is in the open sea, they surround it by creating a sort of carousel, swimming counter-clockwise in two parallel lines or on two fronts moving towards each other.

Once the prey has been concentrated, the bottlenoses dive into this bubbling mass. The range of this circle depends on the size of the aggregation and may vary from 25 to 150 m. Sometimes a solitary hunter attempts to use the same techniques, especially when hunting mullets near the coast.

Another feature that characterizes bottlenose dolphins is the repetitive sequence of jumps, causing loud noises upon impact with the water and forcing the prey in the desired direction.

Research conducted on bottlenose dolphins living in the Gulf of Mexico and along the Florida coast has shown that aggregations are based on age and sex. There are three types of groups: adult males, mothers and their calves, who stay together for 3-6 years, and young males who have not yet reached reproductive maturity. Adult males and females may gather together, while the young males remain isolated until maturity.

G

A

B

C

D

A, B, C, E, F, G - In the bottlenose dolphins, as well as in all the cetaceans, the bond between mother and off-spring is very close and is at the base of the social structure of the group.
The young off-spring can be breast-fed even for 18 months. This long period prolongs the interval between successive births from the same mother to 3-4 years.

D - The small dolphins are still unable to follow the swimming rhythm of the adults and therefore are dragged along by the mother remaining backwards towards the tail.

E

F

G

A

THE KILLER WHALES OF BRITISH COLUMBIA

The killer whale is the largest member of the dolphin family and is a formidable predator in seas throughout the world.

The social behaviour of killer whales has also been closely studied. For over 15 years, biologists from the Nanaimo Biological Station and the University of British Columbia have followed and photographed the social organization of killer whales along the western coast of Canada. They have found two resident communities living in separate territories, and groups of animals in transit, all with specific behaviours. The resident animals are 20% mature males, 20% calves and young, and 60% immature males and adult females. Each community is formed of stable pods of 2 to 50 animals of

B

C

all ages and both sexes, with the mature male the identifying element, recognizable by the large triangular fin.

Each pod consists of a family in which the basic unit is the adult female and her calf. If the calves are females, they remain with the mother, even after reproduction, and separate only upon her death, when they form other basic units. If the calves are males, they remain within

the group but are not part of any family.

Resident animals hunt methodically and without fanfare, almost as if they were aware of the abundance of their prey. When hunting, they do not dive more than 100 m, are scattered, but all travel in the same direction, and about 80 animals can occupy an area 100 sq. km in size. They feed primarily on fish. The seasonal variability of food

A, B, D, E - The study of the killer whales of British Columbia has allowed to know this formidable predator better. The entire population is constantly controlled and every single individual is recognised by means of photo-identification. Among the groups present in this area there have also been identified the characteristic sounds of each individual which can be compared to a sort of "dialects".

C - The killer whale, like the pilot whale and the Risso's dolphin present a strange behaviour called spyhopping. This expression indicates when these cetaceans emerge with their head to observe the surrounding environment.

F - The killer whale is a cosmopolitan species which lives in all the seas of the globe. The killer whales of the photograph are swimming near the Antarctic coast.

D

E

F

A

permits an extremely varied diet; during the summer the principal prey is salmon, and killer whales often concentrate on the migration routes of these fish, which are caught during low tide. If there are many killer whales, they work together by surrounding the school of salmon; sometimes an older, more expert animal will emerge with a salmon in its mouth and give it to a younger individual. Other times they will play with the prey for a few minutes before devouring it, much as a cat will toy with a mouse.

The groups "in transit" can travel great distances in a short time. They form unstable groups with various compositions and hunt mostly marine mammals.

B

C

D

A, B, C - The killer whale eats other than salmon, other fish like halibut, large Arctic "sole", and herring. In the stomachs of the killer whales studied during a research campaign there were found 24 species of cetaceans, 5 species of pinnipeds, 1 sea cow, 30 types of fish, 7 species of birds, 2 types of cephalopeds, apart from a variety of other hot-blooded animals and cold-blooded ones like turtles. During the winter it is not unusual that it feeds on seals, sea lions and other cetaceans and one of its favourite preys is the minke whale. There are complex relationships between killer whales and their prey. The hunter can often be seen swimming among a group of its prey without creating any alarm.

78

D, E, F, G -
The male killer whale of Patagonia forces itself onto the beach to hunt the sea lions (D, E). Once these pinnipeds have been caught, they are taken to the females and to the off-spring (F, G). The latter play with the prey before eating them, learning the techniques which they will have to use in the future.

F

G

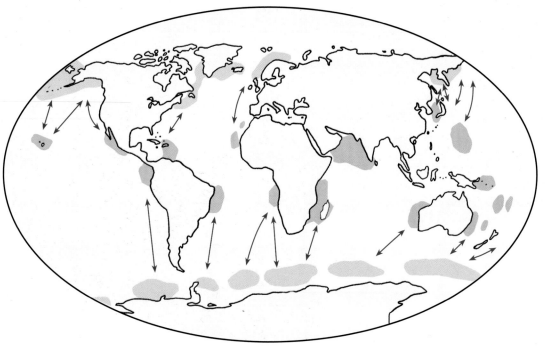

	winter
	summer
↔	*routes followed by individuals from the various subpopulations*

HUMPBACK WHALES

Humpback whales have two large pectoral fins over 5 m long, which make them unmistakable. The ventral portion of the caudal fin has a characteristic colour particular to each individual and acts like a fingerprint, making an exact identification possible. By photographing the flukes of the same individual in areas quite distant from each other, it has been possible to study their migrations, and it has been seen that these animals can migrate for over 9,000 km. The best-known group spends the winter in Hawaii, where it reproduces, and the summer along the western coast of North America, where it feeds. Humpback whales form large herds of up to dozens of individuals, which often change in composition. The most stable social unit is mother and calf, who remain together throughout weaning. Humpback whales reach Hawaii during the winter to mate and give birth. Here the males show off with complex vocalizations, associated with courting and mating. These vocalizations have some basic sounds common to the same population. The "songs" of the humpback whale are used to set territorial boundaries, establish hierarchies among males and as a mating call, and consist of repeated syllables that can form sentences that continue as long 35 minutes. The same rhythm is repeated in an identical manner for some time, broken by pauses for breathing.

During the summer, in the waters of western North America, the humpback whales concentrate on feeding. They have a special hunting system; using their blowholes and moving in a coordinated way, various individuals create a barrier of bubbles to imprison schools of small fish. Taking turns, they dive into the net of bubbles, coming out with an open mouth full of fish.

The humpback whale lives in all oceans. It passes the summer and hibernating seasons in shallow waters near the coast. Migration routes cross deep water. The humpback whales swim at an average speed of a little over 5 km per hour. In winter they move towards the tropical areas, in summer towards the Poles. Due to the de-phasing of the seasons between the two hemispheres, when the southern population is near to the Equator, the northern corresponding species is passing the summer in the North. For this reason any exchanges between the two populations seem to be very scarce.

A, C - The migration of the humpback whales is, among those of the mysticeties, the most well known. In particular, because of photo-identification, it has been possible to observe the presence of an individual in places far apart from one another. For example, it is known that they pass winter in the waters of Hawaii, whereas in summer they move to the waters of the Bering Strait and of the Gulf of Alaska.

B - The impressive form of a humpback whale slides under the bow of a boat in the cold Antarctic waters.

B

C

A, B, D, E - The humpback whale spends the summer in the North Pacific and passes the winter in the warm waters of Hawaii; this has allowed researchers to observe them in particularly favourable conditions. These fin whales are indeed the most photographed of all mysticeti because they swim close to the coast, because they are very curious and, finally, because the water in this area is crystal-clear.

A

B

C - The ventral region of the humpback whale is characterised by large throat pleats, while the fins and snout are characterised by callosity and are often covered with large barnacle crustaceans known as "canine teeth".

D

E

*A, B, C, D, E -
Among the mysticeti
the humpback whales
are those who
accomplish the most
spectacular leaps.
In the photographs
it can clearly be seen
how animals of more
than 35 tons succeed
in rising completely out
of the water, providing
at a demonstration of*

*agility and strength.
The leaps and the
slamming of the
surface with the tail
produces sounds, the
meaning of which is
still unknown. Some
people have suggested
that they are a type of
"exclamation mark"
in the context of a
conversation between
individuals.*

C

D

A, B, C, D, E -
The male humpback whales produce complex and varid sounds. These sounds are associated with courting and mating. It is thought that in this way the males try to attract the females competing among each other to determin the hierarchy for breeding. Courting also involves a sort of dance which the animals perform in synchronization, surfacing and swimming elegantly together despite their size.

E

A

A, B, C, D, E - Humpback whales reach sexual maturity at between four and seven years of age. The off-spring of the humpback whales are born in winter after a pregnancy of 11-12 months in the tropical waters. Their weight at birth is about 2 tons and they are breast-fed for approximately 5 months. After this period they are capable of following the mother in the long migration towards the Poles. Although they are social animals, the most stable relationship is that between the mother and her offspring and may last for over a year. For this reason the females generally give birth every two years and may be nursing and gestating at the same time.

B

C

D

E

A, B, C, D - Among the hunting techniques adopted by the humpback whales, the most spectacular is the blowing of a net of bubbles. This is produced by air emitted from the nostrils to trap and concentrate shoals of small fish. The animals swim from the deep towards the surface in a circular manner and by emitting the bubbles to create a curtain which on the surface appears like a large circular ring with a diameter of some tens of metres. In turn the individuals dive into the net and then swim vertically upwards to emerge with their mouths full of water and food.

Drawing - The "Bubble network" works in the same way as the drag nets used by fishermen to catch blue fish. Seagulls often take advantage of this system but at times they are swallowed in the whales' frenzy, by mistake.

A

B

C

D

THE PARASITES

Parasites are present in almost all organs, in some cases in great numbers; indeed, in other mammals, so many parasites would be debilitating or even fatal. Yet during the course of evolution, the various species of cetaceans and their respective parasites have created an equilibrium that permits the host animal to survive.

This situation is also advantageous for the parasite, which can live longer and reproduce in greater numbers. Nevertheless, when the equilibrium between the host and the number of parasites changes, even cetaceans may die.

We may distinguish endoparasites, which live within the organs and tissues, and extoparasites, which attach to the outside of the skin.

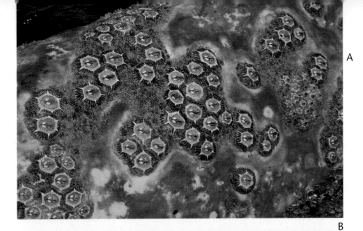

INNER PARASITES OF CETACEANS

SPECIES	Mo	Tb	H	Nc	L	I	Me	Mu	Sk	Sn	P	Lu	K	Cs	B	St
Digena sp.				●	●	●										
Cestoda sp.					●	●	●	●								
Nematoda sp.		●	●			●			●		●	●	●	●	●	●
Acantocephala sp.						●										
Copepoda sp.	●									●						
Amphipoda sp.	●									●					●	

Mo = Mouth;
Tb = Tympanic bulla;
H = Heart;
Nc = Nasal cavities;
L = Liver;
I = Intestine;
Me = Mesentery;
Mu = Muscolature;
Sk = Skull;
Sn = Skin;
P = Placenta;
Lu = Lungs;
K = Kidneys;
Cs = Circulatory system;
B = Blowhole;
St = Stomach.

The table shows which parasites effect the different organs of cetaceans.

E - *Two barnacles of the* Xenobalanus *type have settled on the tail of this speckled Atlantic animal.*

F - *The* Pennellus *is a shell fish so transformed to be unrecognisable, it anchors itself under the skin absorbing nourishment by sucking blood.*

G - *The Cirripeds like* Conchoderma *and* Cryptolepas *reach remarkable sizes compared with those fixed on rocks, thanks to the mobile substratum (the body of the cetacean) which guarantees a constant source of food.*

D

F

E

A, B, C, D -
The crustaceans which live on the skin of the cetaceans assume particular shapes. The amphipod Cyamus scammoni *lives exclusively on the skin of the grey whale, together with numerous cirripeds which characterise the appearance of this species.*

G

Parasites of internal organs include trematodes in the subclass Digena, cestodes, nematodes, acanthocephalae, and others, and each species specializes in certain organs.

External parasites are primarily crustaceans profoundly modified for a sessile life, like the copepods from the genus Pennella. Other species include the cirripeds, isopods and amphipods, which affix to the skin and inside the mouth and the blowhole.

In reality, the acorn barnacles, cirripeds which are most common in mysticetes, are not true parasites, but are rather epibionts, as they take their nourishment from the surrounding environment and only use the host as a surface to adhere to.

A

B

C

D

D - Among the cirripedes, the most common are those belonging to the Conchoderma genus. When they stick to the whales they prefer sheltered places like the whalebones. They possess a sort of peduncle which allows them to raise themselves up to intercept the plankton which nourishes them.

F - The parasites prefer to stick to cetaceans which swim slowly. Some whales, like this grey whale, carry them on their head and on their fins for thousands of miles. On one example 450 kg were collected.

E

A, E - The muzzle and the top of the head of the right whale present callosities on which numerous parasites settle, including amphipods, isopods and cirripedes. These last are shell fish better known with the name of "acorn shells" or "dog teeth". They nourish themselves with plankton and are carried from one end of the earth to the other.

B, C - The Cryptolepas genus of cirripedes settle on the grey whales together with the Cyamus genus of amphipods and acorn shells. The cirripedes do not suck blood from their hosts, but the way they grip on to the skin probably renders them annoying to the host. Their population undergoes seasonal fluctuations: they grow abundantly on the skin of their hosts in the cold polar waters but tend to break off in temperate or warm seas.

F

G - The Cyamus genus amphipod shell fish are also defined as "whale lice". Sixteen species are known and they can reach a length of two and a half cm. They have limbs with hooks with which they anchor themselves on to the skin, mostly around the genitals, the blowhole and other delicate parts like eyelids. The mouth is modified for sucking blood from its host.

G

A

A, F, G - Drift nets, which often spread out for tens of kilometres, often cause accidental death. The smaller species, when caught up, are unable to survive. The mysticeti and the sperm whales have enough strength to remain at the surface to breathe and sometimes manage to get free.

B - Plastic bags represent a serious danger for all the cetaceans and in particular for those species which feed on cephalopeds; in fact, they can be easily mistaken for these molluscs and swallowed, causing obstruction in the feeding duct and consequently death.

B

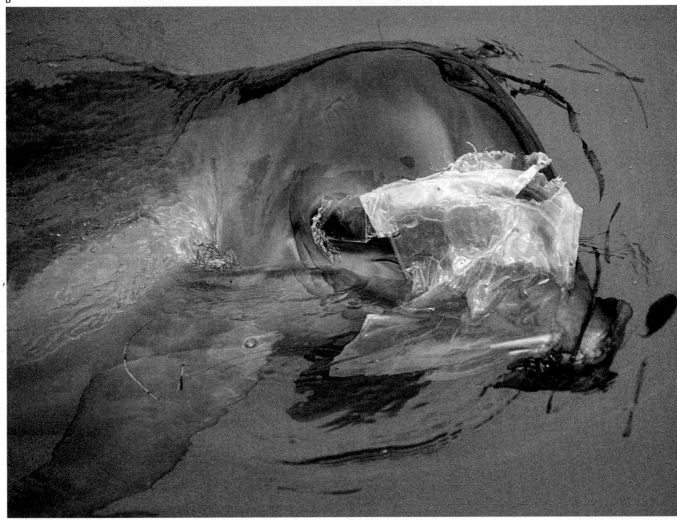

C

D

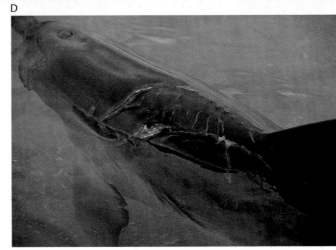

C, D - Sharks rarely represent a danger for cetaceans, however some may attack animals weakened by illness, pregnant females and the young.

E - Narwhal hunting is controlled by the International Whale Commission, but many are accidentally caught up in fishing nets.

THE ENEMIES OF THE CETACEANS

Mortality may be due to natural causes or through contact with humans.

In their natural environment, cetaceans have few enemies.

Sharks may attack calves, the young, debilitated mothers or old and sick individuals. As we have seen, some species, like the killer whale and the false killer whale may eat dolphins, porpoises and sometimes rorquals.

Death may be due to infection or disease, noted especially in stranded animals. Yet the pathologies found may not be the direct cause of the animal's death. Stressful situations caused by catecholamine may cause irreparable damage to the circulatory system. Problems related to heat regulation may cause pneumonia. Metaplasia has been observed in various organs and in the mammary glands. Inefficient metabolism may cause hepatitis. This may also be caused by chemical substances accumulated through the food chain.

Cirrhosis of the liver as well as metaplasia and pulmonary infections may be the result of polychlorurate compounds (polychlorinated biphenyl or PCB, dichlorodiphenyltrichloroethane or DDT and endrin-dieldrin or DDE), pesticides which are commonly used in agriculture; they concentrate primarily in fatty tissues, the liver, and the kidneys, and can be transmitted from mother to calf during pregnancy and nursing. High quantities of these toxic substances in the tissues can also weaken the immune system. This is the case in infections from the *morbillivirus* that caused many strandings in Mediterranean populations of striped dolphins from 1990-92. These phenomena may also occur in larger cetaceans like the mysticetes.

Today, the most dangerous enemy is man, who is responsible not only for chemical pollution, but also for the noise produced by boats, plastic objects thrown into the sea, and a general degradation of the productive potential of the environment. All this may have severe effects on populations of cetaceans, causing death and influencing their behaviour. Direct competition with fishing boats for the same food and indirect resources causes the deaths of thousands of dolphins, without considering the numbers caught each year for food or bait in hunting sharks and "centolla" crabs.

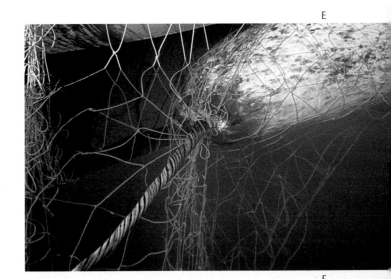

E

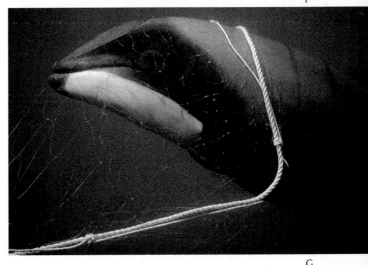

F

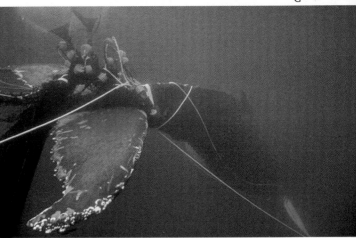

G

Look at the map and relate it to the table to find the general distribution of cetacean species. The numbers and the different colours indicate the subdivision of the oceans in biogeographical areas.

1) Arctic Subarctic
2) North Atlantic
3) North Pacific
4) Temperate Atlantic
5) Temperate Pacific
6) Tropical Atlantic
7) Tropical Pacific
8) Tropical Indian
9) Temperate South Atlantic
10) Temperate South Pacific
11) Temperate South Indian
12) Antiboreal Atlantic
13) Antiboreal Pacific
14) Antiboreal Indian
15) Antarctic Subantarctic
16) Amazon Basin
17) Ganges and Brahmaputra Basin
18) Indo Basin
19) Yangtze Basin

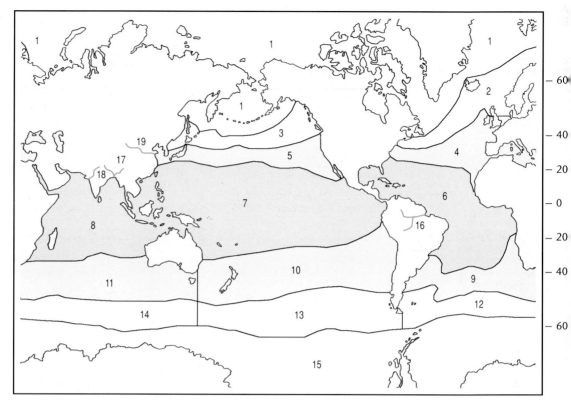

A, B, C - Cetaceans have colonised all the oceans. There exist species which prevalently live in the temperate tropical belt, like the spotted dolphin (A), others which are cosmopolitan like the sperm whale (B) and migrators like the right whale (C), the vital cycle of which develops between the waters of the temperate-boreal regions and the Poles.

THE REASON FOR CURRENT CETACEAN DISTRIBUTION

As we have seen, there are 81 species of cetaceans. Despite the fact that this is a relatively small number and may indicate low differentiation, these mammals can be found in a great variety of environments in all the seas on our planet, and in some of its principal rivers. There are species with ample geographic distribution adapted to life in tropical waters as well as polar ones on both hemispheres, but also extremely specialized species that live in very limited areas with particular climate conditions.

All this is the result of a colonization that began during the great geologic changes, which transformed the oceans and land above water and are even now under way. The current position of the continents and the flows of warm and cold currents may be a barrier to exchanges between populations of the same species which were once in communication. This isolation, which continued for extremely long periods of time (millions of years) has led to the formation of new species and will lead to even more.

The pantropical dolphin lives in the tropical areas of the Atlantic and Pacific oceans, in similar environments and climates. The two populations are separated from each other with no way of communicating, due to the climate barriers caused by the cold waters of Cape Horn and the Cape of Good Hope. On the other hand, while they are morphologically identical, the northern right whale and the southern right whale, which live in the northern and southern waters of the two hemispheres with no way of meeting each other, are considered two different species. Even the

Species	Regions		Species	Regions		Species	Regions
Australophocaena dioptrica	9, 12, 13, 14		Hyperoodon planifrons	9, 10, 11, 12, 13, 14, 15		Mesoplodon stejnegeri	1, 3, 5
Balaenoptera acutorostrata	1, 2, 3, 4, 5, 6, 7, 8, 9, 10, 11, 12, 13, 14, 15		Inia geoffrensis	16		Monodon monoceros	1
			Kogia breviceps	4, 5, 6, 7, 8, 9, 10, 11		Neophocaena phocaenoides	5, 7, 8
Balaena mysticetus	1					Orcaella brevirostris	7, 8
Balaenoptera borealis	1, 2, 3, 4, 5, 6, 7, 8, 9, 10, 11, 12, 13, 14		Kogia sinus	4, 5, 6, 7, 8, 9, 10, 11		Orcinus orca	1, 2, 3, 4, 5, 6, 7, 8, 9, 10, 11, 12, 13, 14, 15
Balaenoptera edeni	4, 5, 6, 7, 8, 9, 10, 11, 12		Lagenorhynchus obliquidens	1, 3, 5			
Balaenoptera musculus	1, 2, 3, 4, 5, 6, 7, 8, 9, 10, 11, 12, 13, 14		Lagenodelphis hosei	6, 7, 8		Peponocephala electra	4, 5, 6, 7, 8, 9, 10, 11
			Lagenorhynchus acutus	2, 4		Phocoena phocoena	1, 2, 3, 4, 5
Balaenoptera physalus	1, 2, 3, 4, 5, 6, 7, 8, 9, 10, 11, 13, 14		Lagenorhyncus albirostris	2, 4		Phocoena sinus	7
Berardius arnuxi	9, 10, 11, 12, 13, 14, 15		Lagenorhynchus australis	12		Phocoena spinipinnis	9, 10, 12, 13
			Lagenorhynchus cruciger	12, 13, 14, 15		Phocoenoides dalli	3, 5
Berardius bairdi	3, 4		Lagenorhynchus obscurus	9, 10, 12, 13		Physeter catodon	1, 2, 3, 4, 5, 6, 7, 8, 9, 10, 11, 12, 13, 14, 15
Caperea marginata	9, 10, 11, 12, 13, 14		Lipotes vexillifer	19			
Cephalorhynchus eutropia	9		Lissodelphis borealis	3, 5			
Cephalorhynchus heavisidii	9		Lissodelphis peroni	9, 10, 11, 12, 13, 14, 15		Platanista gangetica	17
Cephalorhyncus commersoni	9, 12, 13, 14					Platanista minor	18
Cephalorhyncus hectori	10		Megaptera novaeangliae	1, 2, 3, 4, 5, 6, 7, 8, 9, 10, 11, 12, 13, 14, 15		Pontoporia blainvillei	10
Delphinapterus leucas	1, 2					Pseudorca crassidens	4, 5, 6, 7, 8, 9, 10, 11, 12, 13, 14
Delphinus delphis	4, 5, 6, 7, 8, 9, 10, 11		Mesoplodon bahamondi	10			
			Mesoplodon bidens	2, 9		Sotalia fluviatilis	6
Delphinus capensis	5, 6, 7, 8, 9, 10		Mesoplodon bowdoini	10, 11		Sousa chinensis	7, 8, 11
Eschrichtius robustus	1, 3, 5, 7		Mesoplodon carlhubbsi	6, 8		Sousa teuszii	6
Eubalaena australis	9, 10, 11, 12, 13, 14		Mesoplodon densirostris	4, 5, 6, 7, 8, 9, 10, 11		Stenella attenuata	4, 5, 6, 7, 8, 9, 10, 11
Eubalena glacialis	1, 2, 3, 4, 5						
Feresa attenuata	4, 5, 6, 7, 8, 9, 10, 11		Mesoplodon europaeus	4, 6, 10, 11		Stenella clymene	6
			Mesoplodon ginkgodens	5, 7		Stenella coeruleoalba	4, 5, 6, 7, 8, 9, 10, 11
Globicephala macrorhynchus	3, 4, 5, 6, 7, 8, 9, 10, 11		Mesoplodon grayi	9, 10, 11, 12, 13, 14			
			Mesoplodon hectori	5, 9, 10, 11, 12, 13, 14		Stenella frontalis	4, 6
Globicephala melas	1, 2, 4, 9, 10, 11, 12, 13, 14					Stenella longirostris	4, 5, 6, 8
Grampus griseus	2, 3, 4, 5, 6, 7, 8, 9, 10, 11, 12, 13		Mesoplodon layardi	9, 10, 11, 12, 13, 14		Steno bredanensis	4, 5, 6, 7, 8, 9, 10, 11, 15
			Mesoplodon mirus	2, 4, 6, 11			
			Mesoplodon pacificus	7, 8		Tasmacetus shepherdi	10, 13
Hyperoodon ampullatus	2, 4		Mesoplodon peruvianus	10		Tursiops truncatus	4, 5, 6, 7, 8, 9, 10, 11, 15
			Mesoplodon sp.	5, 7		Ziphius cavirostris	1, 2, 3, 4, 5, 6, 7, 8, 9, 10, 11, 12, 13, 14

phenomenon of migrations of mysticetes and some odontocetes such as the sperm whale, can plausibly be explained by the long voyage of colonization that their ancestors began 50 million years ago. On the contrary, species like the hump-backed dolphin, the pygmy killer whale, the rough-toothed dolphin, the melon-headed whale, the Fraser's dolphin and the striped dolphin were not stopped by the cold waters of the Cape of Good Hope, and today are distributed at the same latitude in both the Atlantic and the Indo-Pacific.

THE HISTORY OF CETACEANS AND THE BIRTH OF THE OCEANS

In the chapter on evolution, we provided a general outline of how furry land animals transformed into elegant, streamlined dolphins. Now let us try to use geologic evolution to understand the mechanisms that led to present-day distribution and shaped behaviours and habits.

If we think of what happens during earthquakes and volcanic eruptions, we may be able to barely imagine the spectacular phenomena that caused the continents and oceans to shift during the geologic eras.

Today there is much discussion of the greenhouse effect and what impact global warming could have on the existence of living beings. In reality, the history of the Earth is marked by periods of tropical warmth alternating with cold periods. For an idea of how important this is, suffice it to consider that changes in climate influenced the evolution of new species, the redistribution of others and the extinction of those that did not survive these changes.

Geologic change is a process we cannot perceive, but it is continuous and is still going on today. The divisions of geologic eras and periods as we know them are a human system based on intervals between events or particular situations, similar to the system used to divide history into prehistoric times, the ancient period, the Middle Ages, and so forth. In both cases, due to perspective and lack of knowledge, the more remote periods are the longest.

Two hundred and fifty million years ago, a shallow ocean lapped the shores of the only continent on Earth, Pangea. It is not known if the continental masses began to rise or the sea floor began to fall, but this continent started to break up, forming two continents, Gondwana and Laurasia; a hundred and forty-five million years ago, the division between America, Western Europe and Africa was complete, India was not yet united with Asia, and the Tethys Sea extended over an area that today roughly corresponds to the central Atlantic, the Mediterranean Sea and part of the Indian Ocean; eighty million years ago a fracture appeared between the continental plate of New Zealand and the Antarctic; fifty-five million years ago South America and the Antarctic became two distinct continents; forty-three million years ago Australia also broke off from the Antarctic. During the same period, the Tethys Sea began to gradually but inexorably shrink, and around this time the first cetaceans appeared. For about 15 million years, the Earth's conformation has remained essentially the same.

THE ROUTES OF DISPERSION

With continental drift, new roads opened up. The archaeocetes and the first odontocetes and mysticetes began to colonize the oceans, driven by the need to find abundant food and hospitable places to reproduce.

During the Eocene, the climate was subtropical and the temperature of the seas was uniform. Thus, for the archaeocetes who had evolved in the Tethys Sea, it was easy to migrate and explore the temperate and warm waters of the bordering oceans. The opening in the Caribbean area permitted more evolved archaeocetes to penetrate the Pacific Ocean as well. At the end of the Eocene, cetaceans had already

squalodonts, the appearance of ziphiidae, physeteridae, dolphins and whales. This period is characterized by rising temperatures, followed by a general cooling in the oceans. The isthmus of central America was not yet closed and thus was not an obstacle to the distribution of numerous cetaceans. Species like the gray whale, which spends part of its life cycle in the warm waters of the Pacific, were able to cross it in the Miocene, as demonstrated by the sub-fossil remains found on the Atlantic coasts. As the isthmus filled in, the populations were separated, and today the gray whale is present only in the northern Pacific. The ancestors of the northern right whale probably followed the same route of dispersion.

Table - The distribution of land above sea level, starting from the Eocene (about 65 million years ago), climatic changes and the beginning of cold or warm currents have represented a barrier for all those species the distribution of which is conditioned by the temperature. This phenomenon has favoured or impeded the dispersion.

1) Dispersion of Basilosaurae and first cetaceans
2) Communications routes between the Atlantic and the Pacific
3) Colonisation of the Amazon and Orinoco basins (boto and franciscana)
4) Colonisation of the Ganges and Indus basins (River dolphin)
5) Colonisation of the Yangtze basin (baiji)
6) Corridor of cold currents between north and south Pacific
7) Circumantarctic corridor
8) Corridor of warm currents and colonisation of the north Pacific
9) Corridor of circumpolar warm currents periodically open

A

B

colonized the temperate zones of the two hemispheres. During the first half of the Oligocene, the mysticetes and odontocetes appeared, and the number of species and their distribution exploded, while there was a drastic drop in temperatures and the Antarctic current formed. The complete separation of South America from Antarctica permitted those species adapted to cold waters to cross the Drake Passage from the Atlantic to the Pacific and back.

By the late Oligocene, all archaeocetes were extinct and had been replaced by more specialized forms which were more selective in their choice of environments to colonize.

Another differentiation took place in the early Miocene. Fossil finds have revealed at least 10 genera of

C

D

E

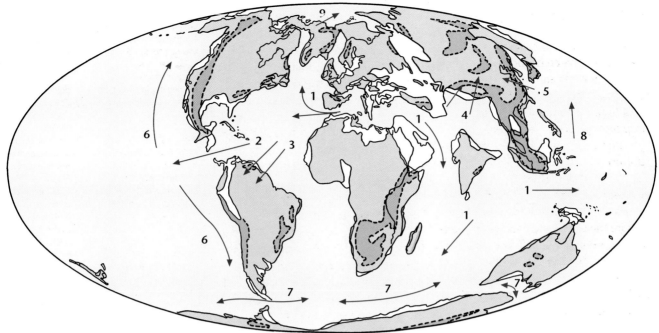

Species more adapted to cold waters could have used the passages at the extreme north and south of the American continent to move from one ocean to another, as some species still do today. On the other hand, the vastness of the Pacific Ocean and the relative lack of islands in the eastern region probably prevented the dispersion eastward of coastal dolphins, especially those that live in the waters of the continental shelf or in fresh water. Even those species that succeeded in passing through faced serious problems due to the cold Peru current, which sweeps northward, and the topography of the western coast of South America, characterized by a very narrow continental shelf and the absence of great rivers like the Orinoco and the Amazon. The only coastal area that can be compared to the warm eastern Caribbean coasts is the Gulf of California with its lagoons.

The Pliocene, about 15 million years ago, is characterized by great climatic changes, with glaciations that brought the surface temperatures of the water down to an average of 6°C. During the glaciations many species dispersed, following circumpolar routes which probably gave rise to the particular phenomenon of migration in which whales and rorquals move between the Equator and the Poles or from one hemisphere to another.

In the Pleistocene the current distribution of cetaceans developed, with the colonization of temperate waters and sub-Arctic regions.

A, C - The dolphins of the Lagenorhynchus genus present an anti-tropical distribution. The Pacific white-sided dolphin lives in the north Pacific (A), the dusky dolphin (C) lives in the southern hemisphere.

B - The right whale dolphins inhabit the northern Pacific and the cold waters of the temperate and sub-Antarctic areas of the southern ocean. The two species which form the Lissodelphis genus, are morphologically separate and this difference could have taken place after the interruption of the cold currents which flowed , during the Cainozoic, along the west coast of the American continent.

D - The hump beaked dolphin genus includes a number of species which have still not been defined to be coastal and of warm water. Two forms seem to be currently valid, one which lives along the north west Atlantic coasts of the African continent and the other, with a wider distribution, from South Africa to the Indian-Pacific area. In this case the separation may occur due to the drop in temperature in the region of the Cape of Good Hope with the introduction of the cold current of Bengal.

E - The origin of the species which today live in rivers, like the boto of the Amazon and Orinoco basin, is probably marine. Like other river dolphins, during the Miocene and the Pliocene (from 24 to 5 million years ago), with the reduction of the sea of Tethys, these dolphins began to colonise the great continental rivers of South America and Asia.

F - Less sensitive species, with regard to the temperature have been able to accomodate the general cooling of the sea and colonise

all the oceans. The minke whale is distributed, with different colouring, from the Arctic to the Antarctic. The photograph shows one of the types present in the southern ocean.

G - The sub-fossil remains which prove the presence of the grey whale in the Atlantic, suggest that this species migrated from one ocean to another when the isthmus of Central America was open. Today its distribution, limited to the northern Pacific coasts, is a residuary of one of its ancestors.

F

G

THE COLONIZATION OF THE OCEANS

A

B

C

A, B, C - Cosmopolitan species like the bottlenose dolphins (A) and the common dolphin (B, C) present a wide difference in the morphomometry of the skeleton and in colour, within the area of origin. For this reason the evolutionary position of the bottlenose dolphin is still controversial. Allthough today only one widely distributed species is believed true, only recently has it been recognised that the common dolphin is represented by two distinct species, Delphinus delphis and D. capensis - separable by the different characteristics of the skull, the colouringn and the average size of the individuals.

D - It has been noted that the Risso's dolphin frequents those areas where the sea floor characteristics render the upwards movements of organisms which live at very deep levels easier. This species hunts almost exclusively cephalopods linivng in submarine canyons, near steep banks or submerged mountains.

The broad geographic distribution of some species like the common dolphin, the bottlenose dolphin, the false killer whale, the beaked whale, the killer whale, the sperm whale and the grampus, or Risso's dolphin, almost all of which are monospecific genera, is due to the presence of subpopulations which were segregated during the Pleistocene by differing degrees of adaptability to variations in temperature within their environment. For these species, isolation has not yet caused the formation of new species as has occurred in other cetaceans.

In some cetaceans, their antitropical distribution has generated two distinct, although morphologically similar, species.

The northern and southern subpopulations of bottlenose dolphins include individuals with the same characteristics, separated by tropical and subtropical forms, with different coloured skins. They were erroneously elevated to the level of species such as *Tursiops aduncus* and *T. gilli*. The current system considers *Tursiops truncatus* to be a single species. The long-finned pilot whale, *Globicephala melas*, has an antitropical distribution, and some writers believe that the southern form is a subspecies, *Globicephala melas hedwardi*. Between these two lives *G. macrorhynchus*, a species which is typically tropical and subtropical. In this case the separation of the species must have taken place in the early Pleistocene.

There are species with an antitropical distribution which do not have intermediate forms in tropical areas. These include the northern rightwhale dolphin, *Lissodelphis borealis*, which lives in the North Pacific, while *Lissodelphis peroni* lives in the southern hemisphere; Baird's beaked whale, *Berardius bairdi*, is found in the temperate waters of the North Pacific, while *B. arnuxi* lives in the temperate waters of the southern hemisphere. The reason for this segregation is probably the interruption, in the tropical region, of the cold current that lapped the shores of western America, flowing north and acting as a bridge across the tropical Pacific, during one of the colder periods of the Pleistocene. This was the path cold water species used to cross from one hemisphere to another. Following this current, which now runs only along the coast of Peru, the penguins reached the Galapagos Islands. Although it is difficult to determine whether the cetaceans headed north or south, it is more plausible that they followed the path of the current from the South. A further confirmation can be found in the fact that the extension of these species into the southern hemisphere is wider and circumpolar, while it is more limited in the North. The absence of a similar current in the Atlantic explains the absence of species like the rightwhale dolphin and the beaked whale in the North and supports a southern origin for these odontocetes, in particular the beaked whales. The discovery of Tasmacetus, the most primitive species of this family, confirms this hypothesis; it is known only through individuals stranded along the coasts of Australia, New Zealand, Chile and Argentina.

The taxonomic difference between the northern bottlenose whale and the southern bottlenose whale, two other similar species with an antitropical distribution, is considerably higher than in the beaked whale. Thus it is probable that their separation occurred even earlier and that their dispersion into the temperate waters of the two

D

E

F

G

H

I

J

hemispheres occurred during the early Pliocene. The porpoise family seems to have spread into the temperate waters of the two hemispheres in a similar manner, between the Miocene and the Pliocene. Porpoises also seem to have originated in the southern hemisphere and to have used corridors of cold water to invade the coastal areas of the northern hemisphere. In this case, the isolation of individual populations caused the formation of different genera, of which the spectacled porpoise is the southernmost. The Burmeister's porpoise lives along the coasts of Peru, Chile, Argentina and Brazil, the vaquita lives in the Gulf of California, and the harbour porpoise lives in the northern hemisphere. The latter is the most specialized and different from other species in the porpoise genus. Fossil remains in Pliocenic layers found in Russia confirm its presence in the North as early as that period. The population isolated by the Black Sea probably formed during the Pleistocene. It includes individuals extremely different from other populations. On the contrary, the similarity between populations of the North Pacific and those of the North Atlantic is so great that it points to a more recent dispersion through the channels of the Arctic islands.

AN OPPORTUNITY TO MIGRATE

A

B

There are species whose distribution during the geologic periods was certainly broader, as fossil remains show. At present, their territories have significantly shrunk and are only a remnant of what they once were. The Cephalorhynchus genus and the pygmy whale are present only in the southern hemisphere. There are four species of Cephalorhynchus, which is one of the most primitive genera, as demonstrated by some of its anatomical features. The narwhal, the beluga and the bowhead whale are examples of species distributed in the northern hemisphere only.

The seasonal movements of these species are confined to the Arctic coasts and seas, with summer concentrations at higher latitudes and a greater dispersal of individuals in the more southerly area of their territory during the winter, depending on the extension of glaciers.

This type of distribution probably occurred during one of the colder periods of the Tertiary and must

have resulted in extremely rapid selection in favour of those species capable of passing their entire life cycle in cold water.

The expansion and retreat of the ice pack following glaciations and interglacial periods influenced the migrations of mysticetes. The gray whale's shift southward is the result of a habit acquired to avoid the ice.

The progenitors of the mysticetes originated in subtropical and tropical regions, more or less in the same areas in which the Bryde's whale lives. During the Pleistocene, they adapted quite well to the cooling of the waters, and subsequently retreated during warm periods to continue to exploit the great production of phytoplankton and zooplankton. These movements still take place today; every year common whales, rorquals and humpback whales make long migrations, moving to summer feeding zones in northern latitudes, but always returning to warm waters to give birth to their young.

The same migratory behaviour occurs in both hemispheres, with a six-month difference due to the fact that when it is winter in the North it is summer in the South. Beginning from a tropical distribution, the mysticetes have followed these rhythms to colonize the cold seas. The result is that right whales and almost all species of rorquals have distinct populations with an antitropical distribution. It is probable that southern populations do not come into contact with northern ones and that only rarely are there exchanges of individuals between one and the other. Indeed, the whales of the northern hemisphere are nearer to the Equator when their southern counterparts are near the Antarctic.

It is interesting to note that individuals of southern populations are larger than their northern counterparts, and that not all individuals make these migrations. Some appear to be more sedentary than others, but in general migratory behaviour in mysticetes is more widespread than in odontocetes.

An exception to the rule is the Bryde's whale, which is thought to have colonized the Pacific through the isthmus in the Caribbean region, which was periodically open. Its movements take place within the temperate and tropical zone.

THE MAGNETIC SENSE

If a man were lost at sea without a compass or stars, he would be unable to find his way back to shore.

Cetaceans, on the contrary, have an extraordinary ability to find their way in seas which appear uniform and void of references, even when they travel long distances. How they do it is still a mystery. Behavioural and neurological studies conducted over the past 40 years have led to a number of hypotheses that theorize the use of various skills such as the directional mechanisms of the sun or the polarization of the light of the sky, smells, infrasounds, ultraviolet light, electrical fields and magnetism.

Only recently has it been discovered that the ability to hear variations in the earth's magnetic field is fundamental, although the sensory system involved in movements and migrations seems more complex. In addition to low frequency sounds, cetaceans can also process other stimuli that regulate the biological clock.

At first the idea that geomagnetic stimuli were involved in orienting marine organisms or that cetaceans could sense geomagnetism was rejected, primarily because humans do not appear to have this sense. Moreover, lack of knowledge on the biophysical mechanisms capable of transmitting this information to the nervous system has always made it hard to support this hypothesis.

C

D

The recent discovery of "magnetotactic" bacteria provided with crystals of magnetite (organized in corpuscles known as "magnetosomas") has helped explain how living beings could use a magnetic sense and the mechanisms for transmitting a geomagnetic stimulus. In theory, a single chain of magnetosomas could provide a whale with an efficient compass, although millions would be required to adequately perceive changes in the geomagnetic field.

Research conducted over recent years has demonstrated the presence of magnetosomas even in migratory pelagic fish. The magnetite seems to be located in the ethmoid region, in tissues full of neuraxons and hair cells.

G - Stranding of groups of the cetaceans seems to be due to route errors caused by the variation of the terrestrial magnetic field. It is now ascertained that in order to travel, these marine mammals follow low density magnetic lines. When these move due to natural causes, they can confuse the cetacean's biological compass.

H - The terrestrial magnetic field varies on the basis of latitude and longitude, the presence of continents and many other geophysical factors. We can therefore trace lines which join together points in which magnetism has the same intensity.

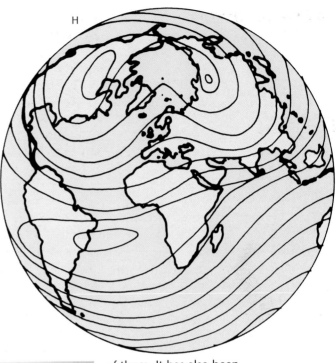

H

E

F

A - The routes that the mysticetes follow during the migrations, can cross different surroundings: from deep sea (as in the photograph), to coastal areas.

B, C - The blue whale lives in Arctic waters up to the Antarctic ice pack. In the southern hemisphere and in the Indian ocean there is a pygmy type, Balaenoptera musculus brevicauda, which reaches a maximum length of 25 m.

D, E, F - The white whale (F) and the narwhal (D) have a confined distribution to Arctic waters and their movements, in general, are a crossing from the open sea to the limit of the polar ice pack, to the coastal areas. The white whale, in particular, prefers to remain in so shallow waters, that part of its body emerges constantly out of the water (E).

G

The use of magnetism is confirmed by the presence of ferro-magnetic material in the tissues of cetacean organs. In addition, structures have been observed in the tongue and integument of the lower jaw of porpoises which are similar to the electroreceptors of fish, capable of noting differences in electric potential induced by swimming through a magnetic field. Paleontological studies have also revealed the presence of magnetofossils, traceable to bacteria 2 billion years old and predating the appearance of eukaryotic cells, which make up all organisms higher than the sponges.

Sensitivity to magnetism may thus be one of the most ancient senses and may be the result of a symbiosis between more evolved cells (prokaryotes) and bacteria (eukaryotes).

Organisms which apparently lack this sense are rare, and for some reason Homo sapiens sapiens is one of them. It has also been demonstrated that animals that live on land have less sensitivity to the magnetic field than those which live in the water.

By comparing the variations in the magnetic field with the phenomenon of mass stranding of living animals, some researchers have theorized that this takes place due to changes in earth magnetism.

Normally cetaceans follow routes which run along low density, low gradient magnetic fields.

The topography of the local field is used as a map which the animals move by, parallel with geomagnetic lines. A timer based on regular fluctuations in this field provides the animals with information on position and distances travelled. Problems may arise when the geomagnetic contours which determine these routes intersect with the earth, or when these fluctuations become irregular, due to instability in the Earth's crust on ocean floors. In this case, the animals are no longer able to use this type of information. If the low magnetism lines overlap on the coast, they cause route errors and can divert the entire aggregation of cetaceans onto the beach. This phenomenon occurs primarily along the coasts in which there are negative variations in the magnetic field.

FROM CALIFORNIA TO THE BERING SEA - THE GRAY WHALE

In winter, gray whales stay in the warm waters of the subtropical zones of the North Pacific to give birth. In the summer they move to feeding areas in the far North, travelling along well-defined routes not far from the coast.

This behaviour is well-known and documented by researchers, who after years of research have identified two subpopulations. The first, known as the California subpopulation, is distributed along the western coast of North America, while the second, known as the Korean group, consists of a small number of individuals threatened by extinction, who live near Korea in the Sea of Okhotsk. A large part of the California population spends the summer, from May to September, feeding in the Bering Sea, the Chukchi Sea, the Beaufort Sea and along the coast of Siberia. In October-November, they begin to abandon these areas and

A

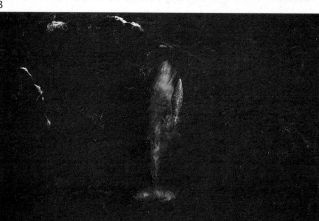
B

A, B, D - The gray whales concentrate in the sheltered bays of the California Peninsula, characterised by shallow warm waters, to give birth. Sometimes, however, the births happen prematurely before the end of the migration.

C - The gray whale is now only distributed in the Northern Pacific but fossil remains indicate that it once also lived the Atlantic.

C

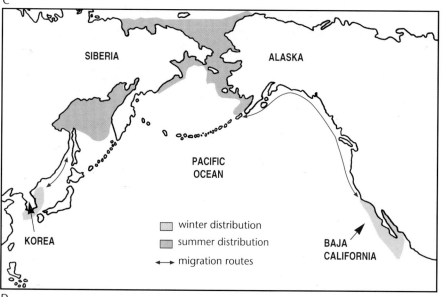

SIBERIA　　　ALASKA

PACIFIC OCEAN

□ winter distribution
□ summer distribution
↔ migration routes

KOREA

BAJA CALIFORNIA

E

D

E, F, G - These gray whales immerse for a short period and then swimming vertically, leap out of the water to fall back, sometimes backwards, on one side or on its belly. The leap is defined in English as breaching. Sometimes the whale rotates along the longitudinal axis of its body to fall on its back, which is more rigid.

migrate south, along the coast of North America, going through the Unimak Pass between Alaska and the Aleutian Islands.

During the voyage, there is a temporary segregation of individuals based on sex, age and reproductive state, which reflects an organized social behaviour. Females in the last stage of pregnancy leave first, and each one generally travels alone. This first group is followed, in order, by fertile females, mature males, immature females and finally immature males. The departures are sequential and involve small pods of two or three individuals.

Most of the whales swim very close to the coast, and in the Monterey area, 94% of the animals passes less than 1.5 km from land. During their movements, they maintain a "cruising" speed of about 8 km an hour and can cover 185 km a day. With this average, in about two months they travel the distance that separates the Bering Sea from Baja California, about 6,000 km. They arrive along the coasts of Baja California in the winter. The females prepare to give birth in sheltered, shallow bays, although some births may take place early, during the migration. For the most part, their young are born from January to mid-February, primarily in the lagoons of Ojo de Liebre, San Ignacio, Estero Soledad and Guerrero Negro. The rest of the population winters outside the lagoons, mostly in the Bay of Sebastian Viscaino and Whale Bay, where most matings take place in December. In mid-February, the gray whales begin to abandon the coasts of California to reach their feeding grounds in the North. This return voyage also follows a precise sequence; the first to depart are females in early pregnancy, followed by non-pregnant females, mature males, immature males and females, and finally mothers with their calves, who leave the reproduction areas about a month after the rest of the group. The first whales reach the Bering Sea in April.

There may be changes in this general scheme. For example, some groups stop along the migratory route before they reach the Arctic. After hunting was forbidden along the eastern Pacific coasts, the whale population increased, making it necessary to extend their feeding area for a more rational exploitation of available resources. While productivity is not as rich as in the Arctic, this is offset by shorter travel distances and a feeding period at least two months longer. On the contrary, individuals who complete the entire migratory route do not reach their feeding areas until the middle of the summer. There are three feeding areas along the migratory route of the gray whales: the lagoons of Baja California, the migratory corridor along the coasts of Northwest America, and the Arctic seas, each of which involves different feeding preferences and behaviours.

F

G

A - The migration route of the gray whale takes it near the coast and in some points they pass it at no more than one km. This whale swims a total of over 6,000 km from the waters of California to those of the Bering Strait and the Cuktchi Sea.

B - The photograph refers to a moment when the gray whale is feeding: it literally "sieves" the sea floor looking for food.

In the lagoons, the whales feed primarily on pelagic species such as crabs, euphausiids, squid and sardines. As they travel, the surrounding environment changes rapidly and their choice increases. They do not disdain an occasional meal of pelagic prey and algae.

In the Arctic seas, the whales can fully assuage their hunger with a true fattening diet. The fatty reserves in their bodies and the layer of subcutaneous blubber increase their weight from 16% to 30%, the equivalent of fully 5 tons. Their preferred menu includes certain kinds of crustaceans known as amphipods. During the summer months, a single whale can eat a minimum of 61,000 kg of these little crustaceans.

This is the only whale that regularly exploits benthic resources, including organisms that live on kelp, although other whales may occasionally feed on fauna from the ocean floor. Their sturdy baleen with its thick plates and large bristles scattered more thinly than in any other mysticetes, are particularly adapted to contact with the sediment.

The gray whale sucks up its prey, swimming on its right side with its mouth near the bottom and keeping its body inclined at about 30°. The food is thus partially separated from the sediment. The finer mud is expelled through the baleen and produces a dense, clearly visible cloud when the whale emerges to breathe.

A

B
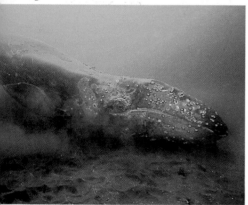

C

D

This activity is of great ecological value, because these whales can move up to 156 million tons of sediment, three times the amount transported by the Yukon River, and cause nutrients to return to suspension, thus stimulating the growth of phytoplankton. In addition, this action prevents the suffocation of the sea floor by mud naturally discharged into the Bering Sea by Alaska's largest rivers.

Overall, gray whales consume from 9% to 27% of the benthic biomass in the feeding area.

Through this wide variety of feeding habits, gray whales demonstrate greater feeding flexibility and more resistance to changes in the abundance of prey. Their diet consists of over 100 types of organisms, both benthic and pelagic, including a vegetal portion, and reflects an opportunistic approach.

Some researchers feel that the presence of algae in the stomach is coincidental, the result of capturing prey living on plants. Others suggest that this ingestion is deliberate. In effect, this material appears frequently and in large quantities in the stomachs of whales, and there are documented cases in which a whale's stomach contained 120 liters of sea-tangles and other algae, along with crustaceans.

Thirty-five percent of stomachs examined by Russian researchers in individuals captured in the Bering Sea were full of algae, and the explorer and whaler Scammon stated that many stomachs of gray whales from Baja California contained fragments of zoostera.

Recently, microbic action within the first chamber of the stomach has been found, which facilitates the processes of fermentation. This seems to make the gray whale a partially optional herbivore.

The migration of individuals in the Korean subpopulation is similar to the Californian one. During the summer, they feed in the Sea of Okhotsk and move south along the eastern coasts of Asia, to the areas where their young are born off the coast of South Korea.

Due to intense hunting, the number of individuals in this subpopulation is very low and probably insufficient to guarantee the genetic exchange necessary to avoid extinction.

E

F

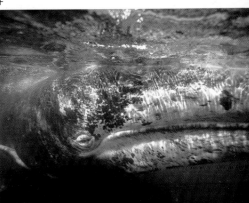

C, D, E, F - The young gray whales (C, D) are particularly curious and perhaps they have become accustomed to being the centre of attraction of the numerous tourists who visit the Californian bays each year to observe these cetaceans close-by. They often remain still on the surface and sometimes allow people to touch them. Apart from their size, the young whales are recognisable by the different proportions of the head and of the body (E, F).

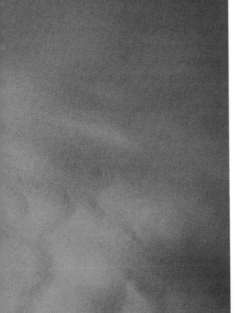

A, B, C, D - The migratory behaviour of the bowhead whale is well known, especially by the populations which inhabit the Sea of Okhotsk and the Bering Sea during the winter and move north to the Chukchi and Beaufort Seas in the spring.

THE KING OF THE ICE - THE BOWHEAD WHALE

The bowhead whale population can be divided into 5 subpopulations, which are apparently isolated from each other. The first travels through the Sea of Okhotsk; the second through the Bering Sea, the Chukchi Sea and the Beaufort Sea; the third through Hudson Bay; the fourth through the Davis Strait and the last through the waters around Spitzbergen.

The movements of this species are based on its permanent residence in

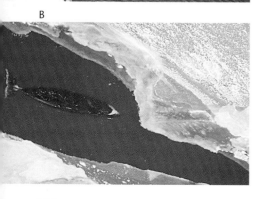

the cold waters of the Arctic zone. The most southerly population is in the Sea of Okhotsk, north of the Sakhalin Peninsula, marking the southernmost limit of its distribution (54° North).

Migrations north begin in the spring, following the retreat of the glaciers, while in the autumn the animals head south, moving away from the returning glaciers. Although they have been known to break sheets of ice 22 cm thick, they try not to become trapped in the ice.

The bowhead whale is extremely difficult to follow due to the environment in which it lives. More is known about the behaviour of the Bering Strait group, while routes followed by other groups have only been hypothesized, and some are known more by their summer concentrations. In general, information is gathered using land stations, or more recently, by small aircraft that make it possible to count and identify them by surveying their transit areas.

E - Of all the mysticetes, the bowhead whale is the species that pushes furthest north. During the summer migration they reach the coastal waters of the Chukchi and Beaufort Seas.

The bowhead whale is capable of crossing frozen stretches of sea, taking advantage of cracks in the ice to surface and breathe or breaking through the pack at the weakest points.

F - The migrations of the bowhead whale take place in spring towards the north, following the retreat of the ice fields, while in autumn the animals turn southwards as the sea starts to freeze. Frequently several individuals move together in synchrony assuming a "V" formation, like the flocks of migrating ducks. This increases the efficiency of hunting their prey, in particular for the individuals which travel on the sides of the formation, in this way they manage to capture the organisms which escape the mouths of their companions ahead or which tend to escape sideways. Such a technique is particularly efficient with zooplankton which is able to move rapidly like the euphausides. These animals always tend to move in perfect synchronization and when they get together in groups operate over an area of several square km.

It has been observed that often a number of individuals will move together, in synchrony, forming a "V"-formation like flocks of migrating ducks. This increases efficiency in capturing prey, in particular for animals traveling at the sides of the formation, who can capture creatures that escape from the mouths of their companions ahead of them or tend to escape sideways. This technique is particularly effective with rapidly-moving zooplankton like euphausiids. As it eats, the bowhead whale moves slowly with its mouth open. Its back generally faces the surface, but sometimes it swims on its side, rotating its body about 60°. These animals, who tend to move in perfect synchronization, gather in one herd to cover an area many square kilometres in size. Aerial observations have shown that, rarely, this species may eat sea-floor (benthic) organisms. Some individuals have also been seen leaving a trail of sediment and mud behind them. As they search for food on sea beds, which are usually a few dozen metres deep, they issue air from the blowhole, causing turbulence as wide as 15 m. The noise this makes lasts 3-4 seconds and can be heard up to one kilometre away. This behaviour seems to be more frequent in the evening and the morning, when food is at its peak.

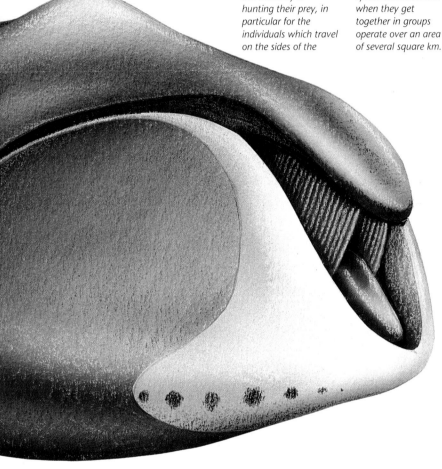

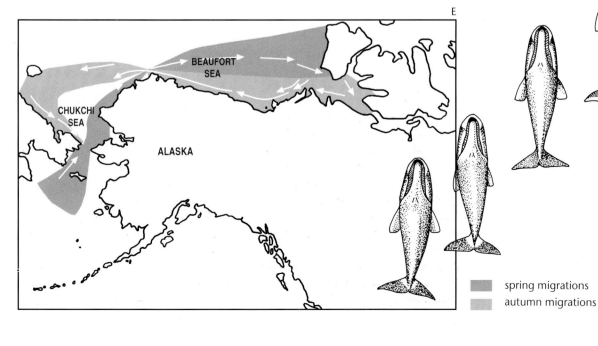

E

BEAUFORT SEA

CHUKCHI SEA

ALASKA

spring migrations
autumn migrations

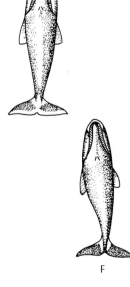

F

THE RIGHT WHALE - A SPECIES FIGHTING TO SURVIVE

Despite the fact that the right whale was the first species to be hunted for commercial reasons and that its exploitation, begun by the Basques in the 10th century, continued until the beginning of the 20th century, it is one of the mysticetes which has been least studied. It is not even clear if the genus Eubalena actually comprises two species – a northern and a southern one – or if

Like all mysticetes the right whale migrates from south to north and vice versa, within the limits of their distribution, to give birth and to feed, but the populations of the two hemispheres apparently never meet, not only because the boundaries of their distribution are 5,000 km apart but also because the seasons are out of phase by six months.

On the basis of fossils found in South Africa, Pilleri and Marcuzzi have suggested that this species originated in the South and that during the ice age migrated towards the equator, an event which could not be repeated

A - The northern right whale lives in the temperate and sub-polar waters of the northern hemisphere and is distributed between 30° and 75° North in the Atlantic. It has also been sighted between 25° and 60° North in the Pacific.

B, C - The huge tail of the right whale allows it to generate a propelling force which can lift its body weight of around 100 tons out of the water.

D, E - A distinctive feature of the right whale is the callosity on the snout. Commensal parasites, amphipoda, acorn barnacles and worms settle on this protuberance whose significance is still unclear. This callosity, which varies in size and position on every animal, allows the animals to be identified and it is therefore useful in the study of migrations and to estimate the number of animals in the population.

A
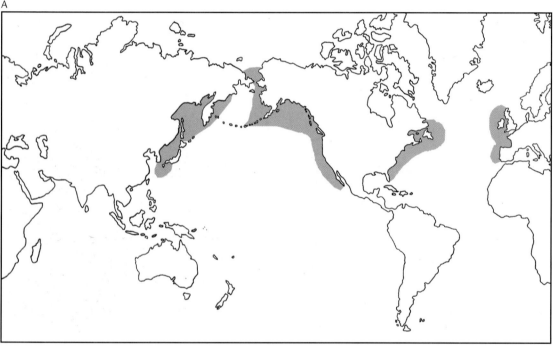

C

the population of the Northern Pacific is formed of animals from one species or different sub-species.

The most well-known of the two is the southern right whale because it is represented by a substantial number of specimens (1,500–4,000) while the northern populations, probably now amounting to only 2% of the numbers living before they were commercially caught, find it difficult to recover and build up their numbers, even if hunting is strictly forbidden.

The northern right whale can now be found between 30° and 75° north in the Atlantic but proof exists that in the past they also lived in the Gulf of Mexico and between 25° and 60° north in the Pacific.

The southern right whale is found between 20° and 60° south throughout the Southern hemisphere.

B

D

E

because of the rise in temperature.

The routes followed by the right whale are mostly unknown; it is thought that the group found along the coasts of north-west America in winter, in summer migrates to the Davis Strait and offshore Greenland.

In the Pacific the animals migrate from the Yellow Sea and the Sea of Okhotsk on the Asiatic coasts and from the coasts of Oregon in America to the Bering Strait to the islands of St. Matthew, St. Lawrence and to Cap du Prince de Galles in Alaska.

In the Southern hemisphere the most studied group is the one which spends the winter close to the Valdés peninsula; it comprises around 1,200

A, B, D - The population renewal of the northern right whale, after the prohibition to hunt fixed by the International Whale Commission in 1935, seems to be very slow and their rarity renders ever more difficult to follow their movements and therefore define their distribution. Sometimes chance sightings such as that which occurred in 1997 in the Meditteranean confirm that this species is re-colonising its past areas.

C - In order to feed, the right whale uses echo-location or listens to the sound produced by krill. In certain cases it remembers where it hunted previously and heads to areas in which its prey is abundant.

E - Perhaps the most curious behaviour of the right whale is its "sail" propulsion. Payne observed for the first time in 1986 that individuals of this species used the caudal fin to be pushed by the wind.

D

E

A

B

C

animals which move to the Antarctic peninsula every summer to feed on krill. It has recently been noted that the number of specimens which winter off Australia and New Zealand has increased in some cases at a rate of 5% or even 16%.

The animals migrate along three main routes: from Western Australia to New Zealand towards the Dumont d'Urville Sea and the Scott Sea in the Antarctic. For the right whale Antarctic waters represent an important feeding ground, the main prey is crustaceans such as *Euphausia superba* and pelagic larvae and the *Munida gragaria* galateide crab, but fish and calanus can take on a dominant role in some zones.

F

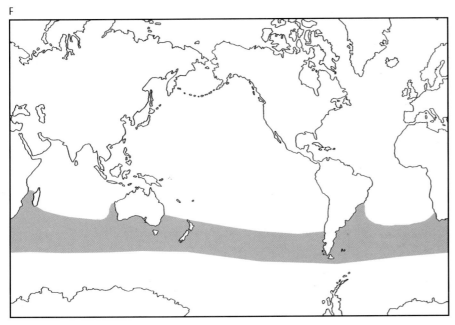

F - The feeding grounds of the southern right whale, which were more extensive than at present, are located to the south of the southern continents as far as the Antarctic peninsula.

G, H, I - An important part of the population of this species winters along the Southern coasts of Australia where the young, characterised by lighter colours, are born in shallow water and sheltered bays.

G

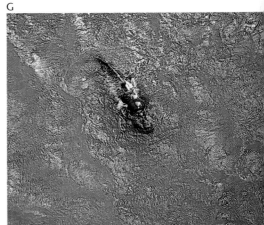

H

I

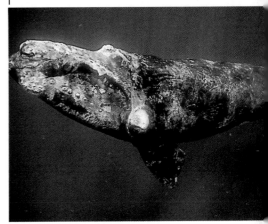

A

B

C

D

E

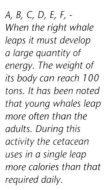

*A, B, C, D, E, F, -
When the right whale
leaps it must develop
a large quantity of
energy. The weight of
its body can reach 100
tons. It has been noted
that young whales leap
more often than the
adults. During this
activity the cetacean
uses in a single leap
more calories than that
required daily.*

F

A

B

A WHITE DOLPHIN, THE BELUGA

The life cycle of the beluga includes seasonal migrations along the coasts of the Arctic seas. Movements are regular, although not for long distances, and are affected by various factors: the formation of ice, changes in food distribution and weaning of calves.

This species has a particular predilection for shallow waters and can swim where the water is so shallow that it only covers part of its body. Nevertheless, the beluga has been seen to reach depths of over 600 m. This stratagem gives it numerous advantages.

With its skin exposed to the sun, it needs to expend less energy to regulate temperature; swimming in shallow waters helps it elude predators like the killer whale; and finally, during certain seasons it can find abundant prey in the estuaries.

Belugas travel in pods, with subgroups formed by females with calves, separated from mature males. During the summer migration, the oldest members of the group lead the way to the estuaries, while the rest of the group stays in the open sea.

The beluga's diet is a typical example of adaptation to the productivity of the Arctic seas and is extremely varied, although like other predators such as the narwhal and some seals, it prefers benthic species such as fish, mollusks and other invertebrates.

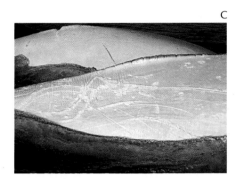

C

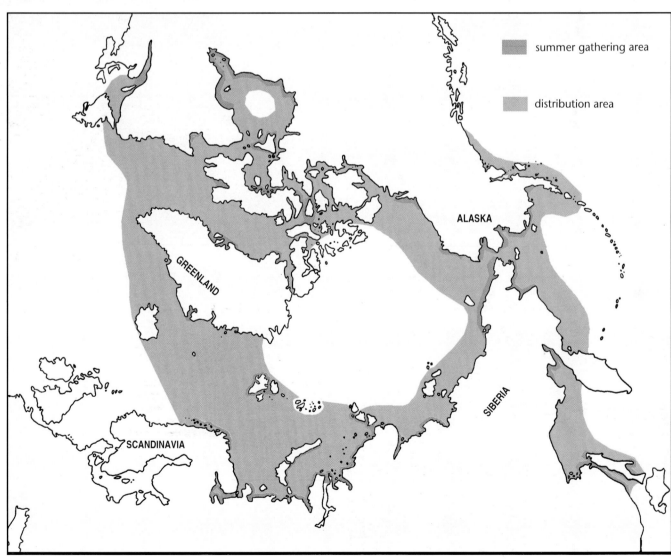

summer gathering area

distribution area

ALASKA

GREENLAND

SIBERIA

SCANDINAVIA

A, B, C, D, E, F, -
To abandon itself to the pleasure of scratching its body against the rounded rocks, at the end of the river outlets and to dry in the sun may be dangerous for the white whale. The seasonal cleaning of the skin which must be renewed and the necessity to stay in shallow waters to give birth brings the white dolphins from the Arctic to enter into the estuaries every year. The arrival of low tide occasionally takes some individuals by surprise and they are left high and dry, keeping still to wait for the high tide to escape.

D

E

F

Map - The presence of the white whale in Arctic waters is ruled by the extension of the ice pack, its northern boundary during winter coincides with the southern one of the polar ice pack. During the summer these species migrate to the coast in well defined and noted areas. The map shows the general distribution of the species in blue while the summer habitat is shown in red.

A

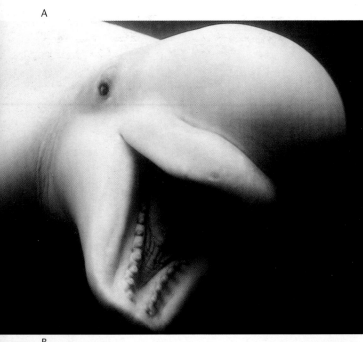

A, B, C - The white whales feed on invertebrata which live in the sand. The particularly mobile lips allow them to enjoy this type of nourishment, uncommon to the other carnivorous whales. This strategy allows them to exploit the abundant resources of the Arctic seas.

D, E, F, G - During their movements and hunting activity, the white whales keep constantly in contact with each other by communicating with sounds and whistles of short periods (50-80 ms) and at frequencies of about 100 KHz.

E

B

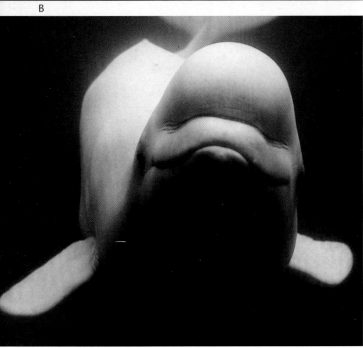

C

D

F

G

THE SPERM WHALE, LORD OF THE OCEANS

The sperm whale is the largest of the odonocetes; adult males can exceed 18 m in length and weigh up to 50 tons, while females are smaller, about 12 m long, and reach a weight of about 20 tons.

The sperm whale is a cosmopolitan species and lives in all oceans of the world. Nevertheless, only males reach the highest latitudes, while females tend to be more sedentary. The territory of the males extends from the Antarctic glaciers to the 75° parallel North, while females remain within the 50° parallel of the two hemispheres.

The populations are partially isolated from each other, but exchanges can take place, for both sexes, between the Atlantic Ocean and the Indian Ocean around the Cape of Good Hope (35° South) and between the Pacific Ocean and the Indian Ocean through the Sunda Strait and south of Tasmania (43° South). Only males cross Cape Horn (57° South), which joins the Atlantic with the Pacific.

With regard to exchanges in the populations of the two hemispheres, only one such case is known, when a marked animal crossed the Equator. Our knowledge of the distribution of the sperm whale in all oceans comes mostly from the log books of American whaling ships that hunted this species until the late 1800's.

The general migration pattern is similar to that of rorquals. During the winter, the animals move to warmer waters near the Equator to reproduce, while in the summer they migrate to the Poles to reach their feeding areas.

The social organization of this creature is quite complex and structured into separate groups based on state of sexual maturity. There are essentially two types of groups: reproductive groups and bachelor groups. The first always contain females of all ages and young males, and may include from four to over a hundred individuals. One or a few adult males joins this group only during the mating season, while the young males leave shortly before reaching maturity, between 18 and 21 years old. The bond between the females and the rest of the individuals is quite close, and based on studies in which individuals are marked, it has been seen that some females stay in the same group for over 10 years.

The bachelor group consists of males only, of the same age and size. The smallest and youngest form larger groups than those of sexually mature males, while the largest and oldest males usually become solitary.

Generally the group swims near the surface at a speed of about 8 km an hour, although when in danger, these animals can reach up to 30 km an hour. When the sea is calm, it is not uncommon to see large individuals immobile on the surface.

Only beaked whales can rival them in diving ability and duration. Normally they can reach over 1,000 m in depth and can stay on the sea floor for over an hour without breathing, but exceptionally long dives of over two hours have been noted, reaching depths of about 3,000 m.

Hunting techniques can only be imagined, as it has never been possible to directly observe animals hunting. Studies of gastric contents show that luminous prey represents 97% of their diet, and it has been deduced that they feed primarily at night and, due to their amazing diving abilities, at great depths as well. In the total darkness, their prey may not see them, making it possible for them to come close enough to

A

B

A, C - Only the female and the immature male sperm whale are gregarious. In general these individuals do not frequent the high latitudes, but remain in the temperate and tropical belt. The mature males are generally solitary and they move to the extremes of their distribution.

B - When the sperm whale immerses it raises its tail vertically; the course that it follows under water is practically vertical and even though it reaches considerable depths and remains on the sea floor for a long period, it re-emerges at the same point.

Drawing - The cephalopods form the principal nourishment of the sperm whale in all the oceans, however in each zone the diet composition of the cetacean varies.

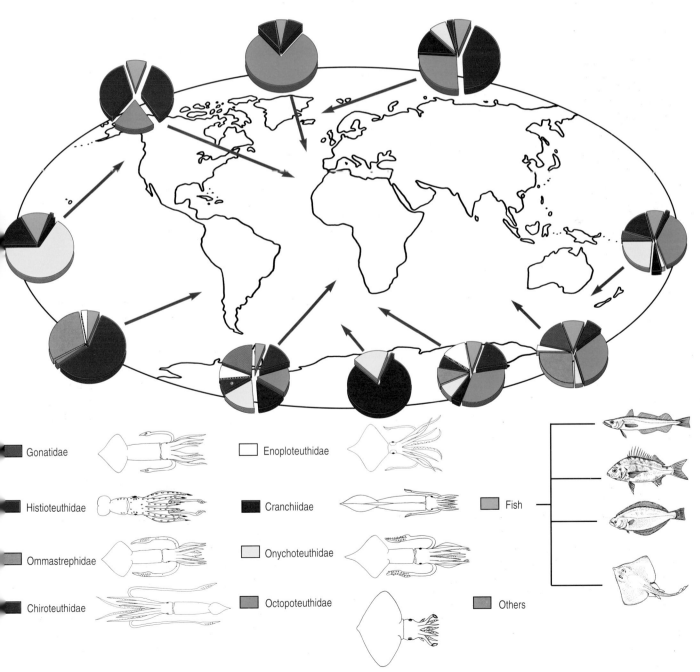

Gonatidae

Histioteuthidae

Ommastrephidae

Chiroteuthidae

Enoploteuthidae

Cranchiidae

Onychoteuthidae

Octopoteuthidae

Fish

Others

touch them with their open mouth. This could explain the fact that sperm whales have been found dead because they have become entangled in underwater electrical cables.

The use of echolocation is plausible, but it has not yet been completely proved. It has been theorized that the sperm whale does not hunt actively, but remains immobile on the ocean floor, using a technique similar to an underwater ambush. The white spots around the mouth may attract prey and be useful for this technique. In addition, according to some researchers, the spermaceti organ in its enormous head may help it to control its weight. By regulating the water entering through its nostrils, it cools the oil which makes up this organ and increases its density at will. The sperm whale can thus dive more easily and remain motionless at the desired depth, as it waits for a luminous squid to pass within reach of its jaws. Not everyone agrees with this hypothesis, and some believe that this enormous animal simply uses its sight to identify prey.

It has 40 to 52 teeth per jaw, up to 10 cm in diameter. Despite the fact that their teeth are numerous and strong, researchers do not believe that they are used to grasp prey, and some evidence supports this theory.

Young sperm whales begin to feed on squid and fish before they teethe, and when prey is found in the stomachs of adults, it is rarely chewed

B

A

up, but is usually sucked in and swallowed whole. The presence of throat pleats confirms this theory. Thus, its teeth are used only to immobilize larger prey.

We have a great deal of information on the diet of sperm whales, making it possible to draw comparisons with various geographical areas. In general, fish are secondary to cephalopods and include various nektonic and benthic species. They are often quite large, like tuna, barracuda and shark. An extreme example is the 2.5 m-long elephant shark *(Cetorhinus maximus)* found in the stomach of an individual caught in the Azores.

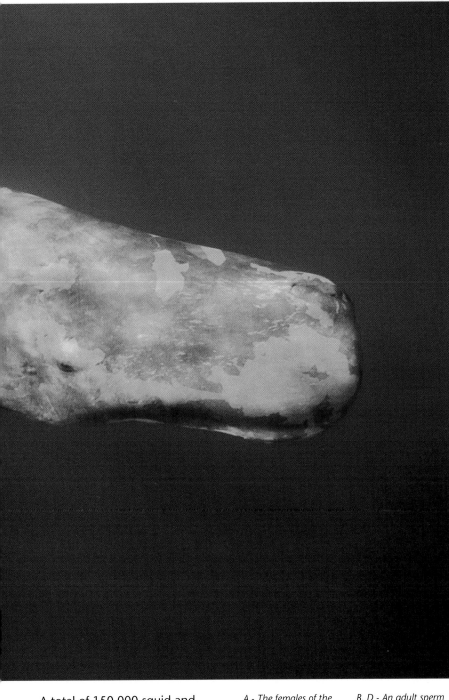

A total of 150,000 squid and octopuses have been found in sperm whale stomachs examined by researchers, more than all the samples of cephalopods conserved in scientific collections in the world.

The relative importance of each species varies if we consider number or weight. The average weight of a cephalopod varies from 0.6 to 8 kg. Considering that there are at least 85,000 sperm whales in the Antarctic and that cephalopods comprise 95% of their diet, it can be estimated that they utilize 12 million tons in a period of about 120 days, the usual time they remain in these cold waters.

A - The females of the sperm whales often assume a characteristic position called "marguerite" probably for defence. To do this they get close to one another with their muzzle and seem to be housewives exchanging secrets.

B, D - An adult sperm whale has few enemies in his surroundings, but the young ones, which at birth are about 4 m long, may be an easy prey to killer whales and big sharks. For this reason they constantly follow the mother and protect themselves under her enormous body.

C, E - The colour of the skin of the sperm whale is not uniform, but its skin presents white marks around the mouth, on its sides and on its belly and lighter and darker areas are due to the renewal of the skin. The entire body, with the exception of the head, is covered by numerous wrinkles and tubercles. Often there are scars due to fighting between males or to encounters with big squids with hooked tentacles; there are visible on its sides and around its mouth.

C

D

E

THE BLIND RIVER DOLPHIN

Life in the murky waters of the Ganges has changed the morphology of this dolphin, which differs from marine species in two significant ways. First, it has an especially long jaw, and second, its visual abilities are reduced. The elongated rostrum can reach one fifth of its body length and resembles a pair of surgical tweezers. Both jaws have numerous small teeth that are visible even when its mouth is closed. It has wide fins that facilitate swimming on its side and probably perform a tactile function, useful for exploring the river bottom. Its free cervical vertebrae allow the head to move independently, while its dorsal fin is scarcely visible.

The systematics of this river dolphin are controversial, and many attribute two species to the Platanista genus, the Ganges river dolphin (*P. gangetica*) and the Indus river dolphin (*P. minor*), while others assert that these are only two subspecies.

The territory of the river dolphin along the river system of the Ganges and the Brahmaputra is bounded to the North by the Narayani and Mahakali tributaries in Nepal, 250 m above sea level, to the East by the

A - The River dolphin is known for two species, the Indus River dolphin, which is distributed along the main course of the Indus and of its tributaries, in the Sind province of Pakistan and the Ganges River dolphin which lives in the group of rivers Ganges, Brahmaputra, Meghna and Karnaphuli, in India.

B, C - The two populations of the River dolphins are geographically separate but the animals have very similar characteristics and differ only by size, the Indus River dolphin is smaller than the Ganges one (B, C). They are species endangered by many perils. Many rivers inhabited by these dolphins are obstructed by dams for producing electricity and the animals remain isolated during the mating season. Moreover chemical pollution, sea traffic and fishing are increasing. It is extremely difficult to photograph them due to the environment in which they live.

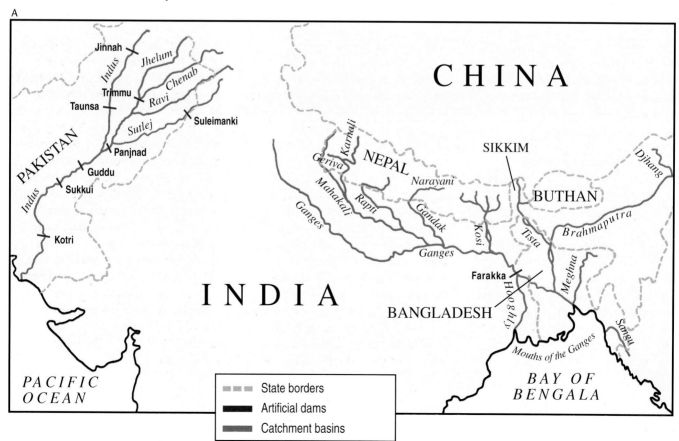

State borders

Artificial dams

Catchment basins

126

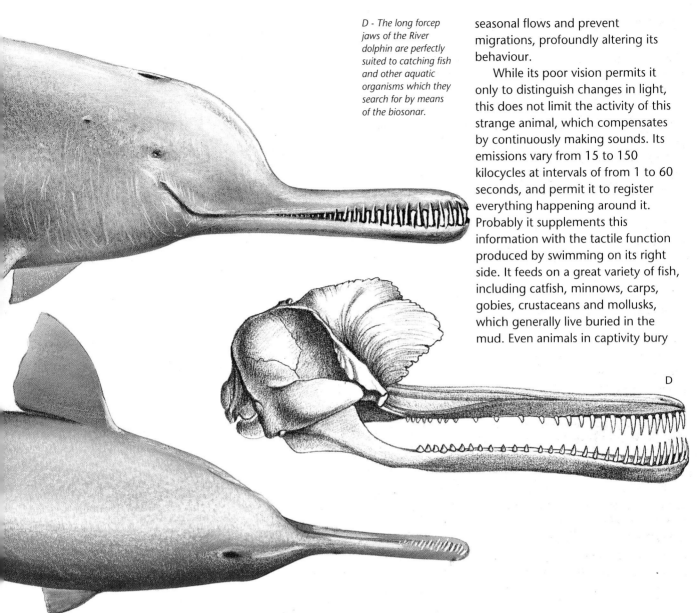

D - The long forcep jaws of the River dolphin are perfectly suited to catching fish and other aquatic organisms which they search for by means of the biosonar.

D

seasonal flows and prevent migrations, profoundly altering its behaviour.

While its poor vision permits it only to distinguish changes in light, this does not limit the activity of this strange animal, which compensates by continuously making sounds. Its emissions vary from 15 to 150 kilocycles at intervals of from 1 to 60 seconds, and permit it to register everything happening around it. Probably it supplements this information with the tactile function produced by swimming on its right side. It feeds on a great variety of fish, including catfish, minnows, carps, gobies, crustaceans and mollusks, which generally live buried in the mud. Even animals in captivity bury

Lohit River in the Indian province of Assam, to the mouths of the rivers that constitute the broad delta, but not to salt water. In Bangladesh it lives in the Karnapuli River, which it probably reached by following the fresh water flow of the Ganges into the sea at the Bay of Bengal.

Along the Indus River, the river dolphin lives primarily between the Sukkur and Guddu dams, located about halfway down its course. The rest of the population is above and below this point, up to about 10 km from the sea. The seasonal changes in its distribution and its concentration in certain areas are primarily due to fluctuations in water level. During the dry season, from October to April, the dolphins leave the secondary

tributaries for the major rivers, and then expand their territory once again with the next rainy season. Only the youngest individuals remain in the secondary channels during the dry season. During this period, some of them may be cut off in the pools and little lakes that form.

It can live in a wide temperature range, from 8° to 33°C. Today the river dolphin is considered an endangered species. This is due to the numerous dams being constructed, which become insurmountable obstacles to the waterways in which it lives. Thus, individuals are cut off with almost no way of meeting again, especially during the reproductive period. Moreover, these dams change the

their beaks in the sediment in search of food. Normally the river dolphin grabs its prey by the head. If the hold is not right, it lets go and grasps it again in the proper position. If the fish is particularly large (over 30 cm), the dolphin carries its prey to the surface and shakes it vigorously, holding on very tightly. Some individuals have even been seen grabbing ducks which were sifting through the bottom in search of food. The river dolphin is not a very social animal and hunts alone, only rarely collaborating with other individuals. It is curious to note that there is a singular physiognomic similarity between the snout of this dolphin and that of the gavial, a crocodile that lives in the same environment.

THE CETACEANS
MYSTICETES: CETACEANS WITH BALEEN

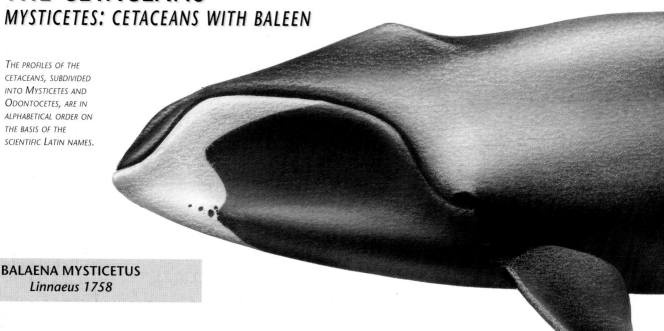

BALAENA MYSTICETUS
Linnaeus 1758

- **Common names: En:** bowhead whale; **Fr:** baleine du Groenland; **Sp:** ballena de cabeza arqueada; **It:** balena della Groenlandia
- **Significance of scientific name**
balaena = whale; *mysticetus* = with whiskers
- **Some data**
Maximum length: 20 m for females and 18 for males;
Adult weight: 75 - 100 t;

Life span: 40 years;
Gestation period: 12 - 16 months;
Length at birth: 4 - 4.5 m;
Lactation: 12 months;
Birth interval for the same mother: 3 - 6 years;
Mating season: spring;
Duration of dives: 30 min.;
Diving depth: 1,100 -1,200 m (adults), 732-1,097 m (young);
Maximum speed: 20 Km/hr

- **Curious facts:** Has 340 baleen plates on each side of the jaw and each plate may reach 4.3 meters in length, longer than any other mysticete.
- **Distribution:** Lives in cold waters in the northern hemisphere. Whalers and Inuit could distinguish different "types" of this whale based on size, skeletal structure, body colour, length and colour of baleen. These differences have been confirmed by

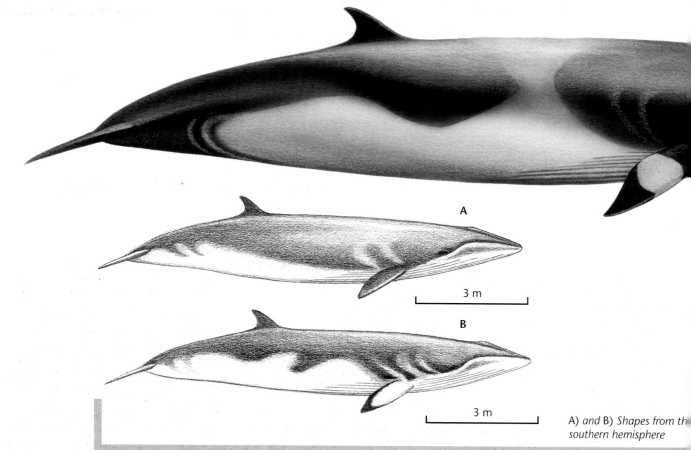

A) and B) Shapes from the southern hemisphere

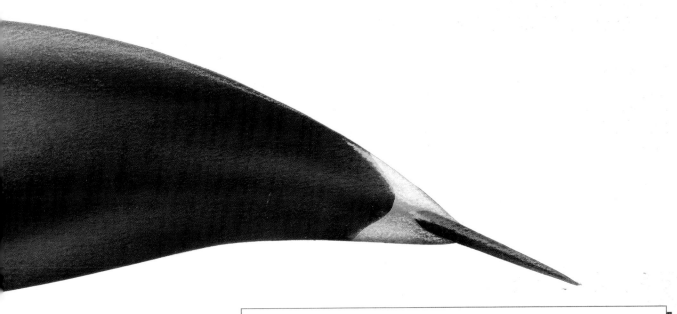

recent genetic analyses as well, but due to scarcity of specimens, it still cannot be confirmed that the Balaena genus includes more than one species. The western Atlantic stock is estimated to be between 25% and 77% of its size before whaling; it is increasing by about 2% - 3%. The Inuit killed 57 individuals in the 1995-96 season.

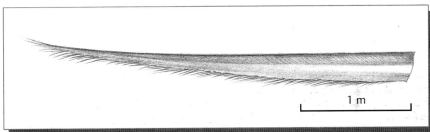

1 m

BALAENOPTERA ACUTOROSTRATA
Lacépède, 1804

Northern specimen

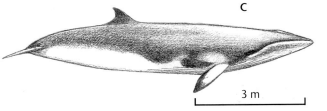

C

C) Pygmy subspecies

3 m

- **Common names: En**: minke whale; **Fr**: petit rorqual; **Sp**: rorcual enano; **It**: balenottera minore
- **Significance of scientific name**
Balaena = whale, *pteron* = fin; *acutorostrata* = with sharp rostrum
- **Some data**
Maximum length: 10.7 m females and 9.8 m males;
Adult weight: 14 t;
Life span: 30 - 50 years;
Age reaches sexual maturity: 7 years females and 6 years males;
Gestation period: 10 months;
Length at birth: 2.4 - 2.8 m;
Weight at birth: 400 Kg ;
Lactation: 4 - 5 months;
Mating season, northern hemisphere: October - March;
southern hemisphere: June - December;
Length of dives: 20 min.;
Maximum speed; 30 Km/hr
- **Distribution**: Lives from the poles to the tropics, preferring the open sea. Two subspecies have been identified, one of which is a pygmy that does not exceed 7.5 m in size and lives in the waters of South Africa and Australia. After strong pressure to reopen whaling for this species, in 1994 Norway received permission to whale for scientific purposes. According to IWC data, in the 1995-96 season, 163 individuals were killed by Denmark, 218 by Norway, 100 by Japan in the North Pacific and 440 in the Antarctic, where an international whale protection sanctuary was established in 1994.

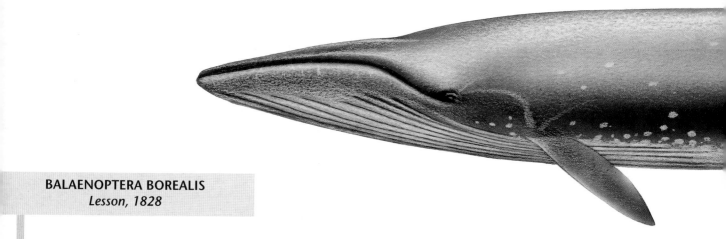

BALAENOPTERA BOREALIS
Lesson, 1828

• **Common names: En**: sei whale;
Fr: rorqual de Rudolphi; **Sp**: rorcual del
norte; **It**: balenottera boreale
• **Significance of scientific name**
Balaena = whale, *pteron* = fin,
borealis = northern
• **Some data**
Maximum length: 20 m for females
and 17.7 for males;
Adult weight: 30 t;
Life span: 60 years;
Age reaches sexual maturity; 8 - 11 years;

Gestation period: 10.5 - 12 months;
Length at birth; 4.5 m;
Weight at birth: 650-800 kg;
Lactation: 5 - 9 months;
Mating season: April - August;
Length of dives: 20 min.;
Diving depth: 300 m;
Maximum speed; 25 Km/hr
• **Distribution:** The sei whale is present in
all oceans in the world, although it prefers
surface temperatures between 8° C
and 25° C.

Rudolphi first described this species in
1822 and called it *Balaena rostrata,* but in
1823 Cuvier recognized the difference
from the Balaena genus, which also has no
throat pleats, and called it the "Northern
rorqual." In 1828 the French zoologist
René Lesson gave it its present name.
There seem to be two subspecies: *B. b.
borealis*, which includes individuals in the
northern hemisphere, and *B. b. schlegelii*,
those in the southern hemisphere. The
latter are larger in size.

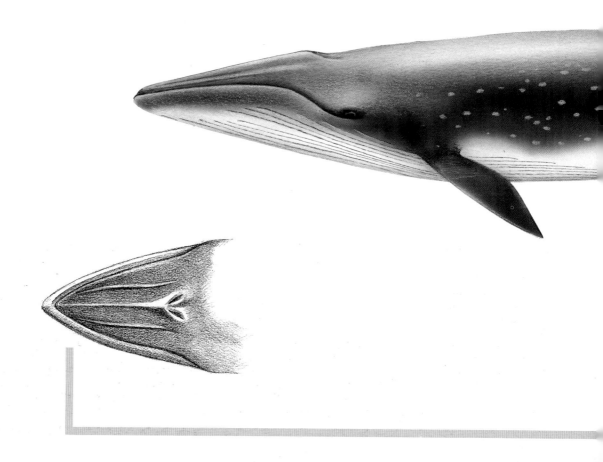

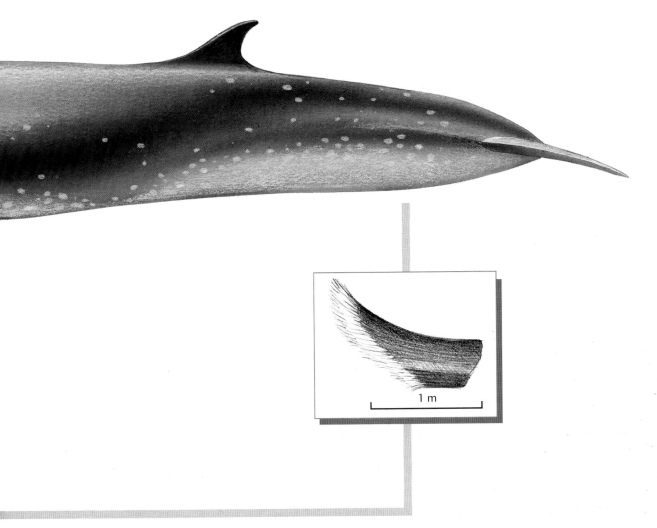

BALAENOPTERA EDENI
Anderson, 1878

• **Common names: En:** Bryde's whale; **Fr:** rorqual de Bryde; **Sp:** rorcual tropical; **It:** balenottera di Bryde;

• **Significance of scientific name**
Balaena = whale, *pteron* = fin, *edeni* = Eden's, in honour of the English commissioner of the state of Burma who brought Anderson the specimen used for the first description.

• **Some data**
Maximum length: 15.6 m;
Adult weight: 25 t;
Life span: 50 years;
Age reaches sexual maturity; 10 years for females and 9 - 13 years for males;
Gestation period: 12 months;
Length at birth: 3.4 m;
Lactation: 6 months;
Birth interval for the same mother: 2 years;
Mating season: all year;
Length of dives; 20 min.;
Diving depth: 300 m;
Maximum speed; 25 Km/hr

• **Distribution:** The Bryde's whale is present in all tropical and temperate oceans in both hemispheres below 30° in latitude, where in general the temperature is higher than 20°C.

For a long time the Bryde's whale was confused with the sei whale (*Balaenoptera borealis*). In 1913, Olsen recognized the difference, but introduced another scientific name: *Balaenoptera brydei*. It was only later recognized that *B. brydei and B. edeni* were the same species. This rorqual has significant morphological differences depending on its geographical area. Two forms are recognized, one with coastal habits and one which is pelagic. Pelagic whaling of this species was banned in 1930, but some coastal stations continued to hunt it until 1987.

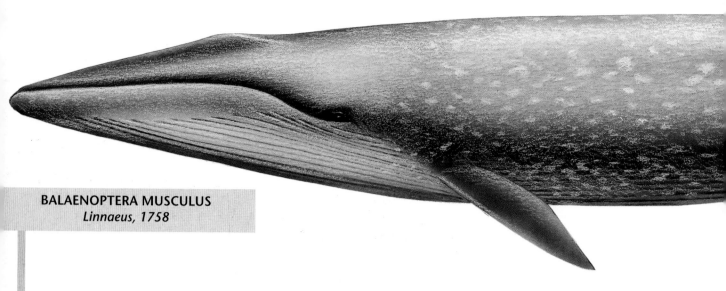

BALAENOPTERA MUSCULUS
Linnaeus, 1758

• **Common names: En**: blue whale; **Fr**: rorqual bleu; **Sp**: ballena azul; **It**: balenottera azzurra

• **Significance of scientific name**
Balaena = whale, *pteron* = fins, *musculus* = muscular

• **Some data**
Maximum length: 33.58 m for females and 27 m for males (24.4 m average for *B. m. brevicauda*);

Maximum adult weight: 190 t;
Life span: 90 years;
Age reaches sexual maturity: 5 years;
Gestation period: 10 - 11 months;
Length at birth: 6 - 7 m;
Weight at birth: 3 t;
Lactation: 7 months;
Birth interval for the same mother: 2 - 3 years;
Mating season, northern hemisphere: fall-winter,

southern hemisphere: southern winter (July);
Length of dives: 30 min.;
Maximum speed: 48 Km/hr

• **Curious facts**: It is the largest living mammal on Earth. The heaviest was a female blue whale weighing 190 tons and 27.6 m long, caught in the Arctic Ocean on March 20, 1947. The longest was another female, 33.58 meters in length, which was pulled ashore at Grytviken, in

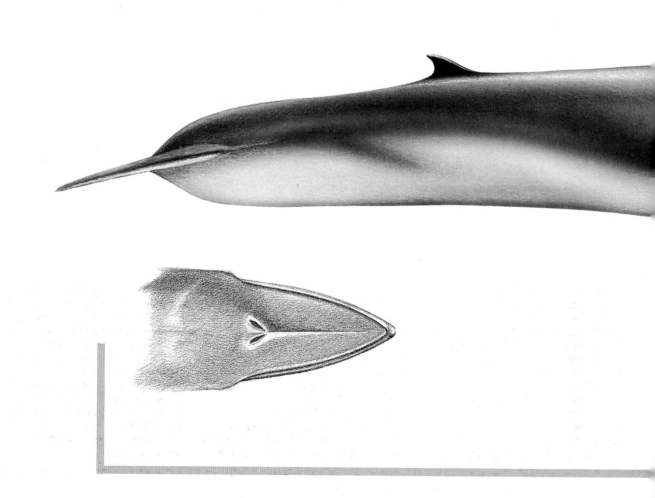

southern Georgia, in 1909. During its first year of life, blue whale calves increase in size by 30 times, and while nursing, the female may lose up to 25% of her weight. Its baleen is the shortest of all whales, only one metre long.

• **Distribution:** Cosmopolitan species. The blue whale population is divided into many stocks. At present three subspecies are recognized, *B. m. intermedia*, which lives in the southern hemisphere, *B. m. musculus*, in the North Atlantic and North Pacific, and the smaller *B. m. brevicauda*, distributed in the subantarctic waters of the Indian Ocean and the Southeast Atlantic. Hunting has been banned since 1964, but it has been calculated that the Antarctic population will require more than 50 years for an acceptable recovery.

BALAENOPTERA PHYSALUS
Linnaeus, 1758

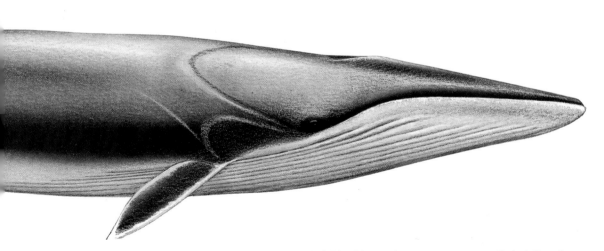

• **Common names: En:** fin whale;
Fr: rorqual commun; **Sp:** rorcual común;
It: balenottera comune
• **Significance of scientific name**
Balaena = whale, *pteron* = fin, *physalus* = refers to the habit of swelling its throat like some anurous amphibians
• **Some data**
Maximum length: 27 m for females and 25 for males;
Adult weight: 80 t;
Life span: 90 years;
Age reaches sexual maturity: 8 - 12 years;

Gestation period: 11 - 12 months;
Length at birth: 6 - 6.5 m;
Weight at birth: 2,000 kg;
Lactation: 6 - 7 months;
Mating season, northern hemisphere: January - February;
southern hemisphere: May - September;
Length of dives: 20 min.;
Diving depth: 355 m;
Maximum speed: 37 Km/hr
• **Distribution:** This species is present in all oceans. Its population is divided into numerous stocks, with various levels of genetic isolation. It appears that Mediterranean fin whales are genetically isolated from the Atlantic population. Some authors recognize two subspecies, as individuals from the southern hemisphere are larger than those from northern populations.

Hunting fin whales has been banned since 1986. Hunting permits are still granted to local populations in Greenland or for scientific purposes in Iceland. Twelve individuals were killed in the 1995-96 season.

CAPEREA MARGINATA
Gray, 1846

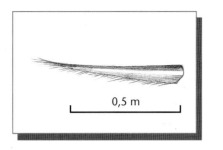

0,5 m

- **Common names: En**: pygmy right whale; **Fr**: baleine pygmée; **Sp**: ballena franca pigmea; **It**: caperea
- **Significance of scientific name**
Caperea = refers to wrinkled appearance of tympanic bone; *marginata* = for the long dark edge on the baleen

- **Some data**
Maximum length: 6.45 m females and 6.1 m males;
Adult weight: 3.2 t;
Length at birth: 1.6 - 2.2 m;
Maximum speed: 9 Km/hr

- **Distribution:** Only one species exists, which occupies temperate waters between 30°S and 52°S. There are no population estimates, but probably it is not as rare as has always been thought.

EUBALAENA AUSTRALIS
Desmoulins, 1822

- **Common names: En**: southern right whale; **Fr**: baleine australe; **Sp**: ballena franca austral; **It**: balena franca australe
- **Significance of scientific name**
eu = true, real; *Balaena* = whale; *australis* = from the southern hemisphere
- **Some data**
Maximum length: 17 m females and 15.2 males;
Adult weight: 80 - 100 t;
Age reaches sexual maturity: 7 - 15 years;
Gestation period: 12 months;

Birth interval for the same mother: 3 years;
Mating season: June - November;
Birth season: spring;
Length of dives: 20 minutes;
Maximum speed; 15 Km/hr
- **Curious facts:** Its body is covered with large calluses; that on the rostrum is called a bonnet because of its resemblance to a woman's hat.

The southern right whale was one of the first species to be hunted; 40 - 45,000 were killed between 1805 and 1844. It has been a protected species since 1935, but was still subject to illegal whaling until 1970. The population's annual growth rate is between 5.2% and 16.2%, depending on zone of distribution.
- **Distribution:** It once lived in all oceans, but now has a circumpolar distribution between 20° S and 55° S.

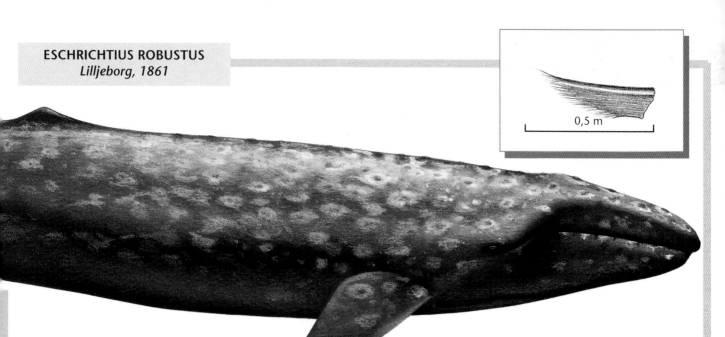

ESCHRICHTIUS ROBUSTUS
Lilljeborg, 1861

0,5 m

• **Common names: En**: gray whale; **Fr**: baleine grise; **Sp**: ballena gris; **It**: balena grigia

• **Significance of scientific name**
Eschrichtius = in honour of the Danish zoologist Eschricht; *robustus* = robust, strong

• **Some data**
Maximum length: 15 m females and 14.6 males;
Maximum weight: 35 t;
Life span: 40 years;
Age reaches sexual maturity: 6 - 9 years;
Gestation period; 13.5 months;
Length at birth: 4.5 - 5 m;
Weight at birth: 500 kg;
Lactation: 7 months;
Mating season: November-December;

Birthing season: December-February;
Diving depth: 120 m;
Maximum speed: 15 Km/hr

• **Curious facts:** This is the whale with the least amount of baleen; it has 130 on each side of the jaw. The size and number are closely related to its feeding habits and the type of prey it prefers.

• **Distribution:** The gray whale was present in the North Atlantic until the 17th century. Its disappearance coincides with the beginning of commercial whaling. Its current distribution is confined to the northern part of the Pacific Ocean. Individuals in the eastern stock have been reduced by whaling (it is believed that at

the turn of the century there were about 3,000 of them). At present they are experiencing an annual growth of 3.2%. Less is known of the situation of the western stock that appears to live from the Korean Sea to the Sea of Okhotsk. It was described as a new species in 1861 by W. Lilljeborg, who gave it the name of *Balaenoptera robusta* based on the subfossil remains found in Sweden. In 1864 Gray introduced the name *Eschrichtius*, first as a subgenus of Megaptera and then as a genus name for the species *E. robustus*. It has been protected since 1946. According to IWC data, between 1995 and 1996, Chukchi aborigines killed 85 gray whales.

■ *The two species, even if living in different areas, have the same shape, livery and morphology.*

EUBALAENA GLACIALIS
Müller, 1776

1 m

• **Common names: En**: northern right whale; **Fr**: baleine de Biscaye; **Sp**: ballena franca; **It**: balena franca boreale

• **Significance of scientific name**
eu = true; *Balaena* = whale;
glacialis = glacial

• **Some data**
Maximum length: 18.3 m females in the North Pacific and 17.1 males in the North Pacific;
Maximum weight: 100 t;
Length at birth: 4 - 6 m;
Age reaches sexual maturity: 10 years

Gestation period: 12 months;
Lactation: 6 - 7 months
Mating season: December - March;
Length of dives: 20 minutes;
Maximum speed: 3 km/hr

• **Distribution:** Some authors identify three subspecies of the right whale: *E. g. glacialis*, which lives in the North Atlantic; *E. g. australis,* in the southern hemisphere, and *E. g. japonica,* in the North Pacific. Nevertheless, at present the accepted species are *E. glacialis,* for northern populations, and *E. australis,* for southern

ones. It lives between 25°N and 60°N. It may be larger in the North Pacific. The right whale gets its name from the fact that when whaling began, it was considered the "right" whale for hunting. This is because it is a very slow animal and thus easy to hunt, but more importantly, when dead it floats, making it easy to recover. The first measures of protection for this species date back to 1935. The last right whales to be killed were in 1967 in the North Atlantic and in 1969 in the North Pacific.

MEGAPTERA NOVAEANGLIAE
Borowski, 1781

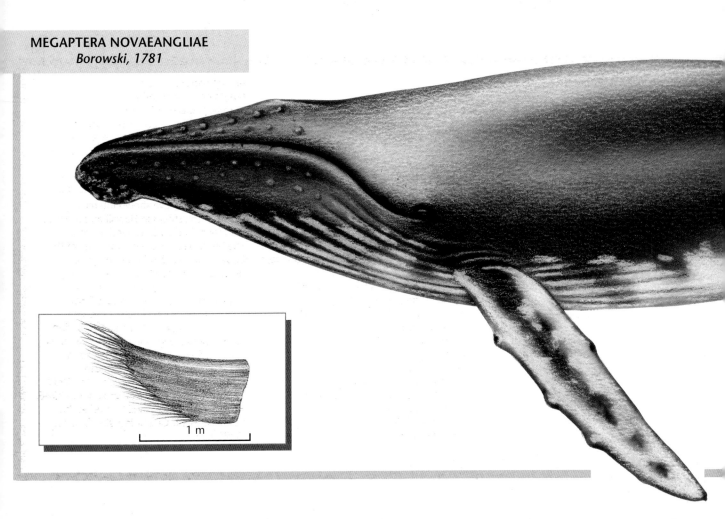

1 m

ODONTOCETES: CETACEANS WITH TEETH

AUSTRALOPHOCAENA DIOPTRICA
Lahille, 1912

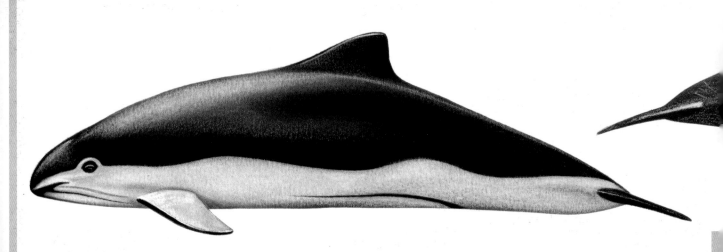

• **Common names: En**: spectacled porpoise; **Fr**: marsouin de Lahille; **Sp**: marsopa de anteojos; **It**: focena dagli occhiali
• **Significance of scientific name**
Australophocaena = southern dolphin, *dioptrica* = from the Greek, optical instrument

• **Some data**
Maximum length: 2.1 m females and 2.3 m males;
Length at birth: 1 m;
Mating season: spring - summer
• **Distribution:** This is probably the most common cetacean in the neritic waters

of Tierra del Fuego, but little is known of its numbers.
Lahille, an Argentinean naturalist, described it in 1912 as *Phocoena dioptrica*, due to a characteristic white ring that surrounds the dark spot around the eyes. In 1985, Barnes reclassified the species.

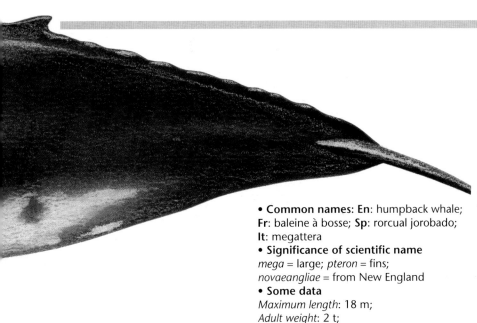

• Common names: En: humpback whale;
Fr: baleine à bosse; **Sp**: rorcual jorobado;
It: megattera
• Significance of scientific name
mega = large; *pteron* = fins;
novaeangliae = from New England
• Some data
Maximum length: 18 m;
Adult weight: 2 t;
Life span: 48 years;
Age reaches sexual maturity: 4 - 7 years;
Gestation period: 11 - 12 months;
Length at birth: 4 - 5 m;
Weight at birth: 2,000 kg;
Lactation: 5 months;

Mating season: winter;
Length of dives: 30 min.;
Maximum speed: 27 Km/hr
• Distribution: Species distributed in all
oceans, from the Arctic to the Antarctic.
It is believed they cannot go beyond the
equator, as the stocks are separated;
populations that live in the north never
meet with those in the south. Nevertheless,
recent studies have shown interchanges
between the stocks in Hawaii and Mexico,
who meet in the Alaska feeding zone.
The humpback whale is a member of the
Balaenopteridae family, although some
researchers believe this species belongs
to a separate family. The population's
estimated yearly growth rate is 9.6% -
13.8%. In the second half of the 19th
century, strong commercial exploitation
of this species began in the North Atlantic,
as new whaling techniques (harpoon-
launching cannon) came into use.
Whaling this species was banned in 1939
in the Antarctic and in other zones in 1966.
Some specimens are still hunted in the
St. Vincent and Grenadine islands in the
Caribbean.

BERARDIUS ARNUXI
Duvernoy, 1851

• Common names: En: Arnoux 's beaked
whale; **Fr**: béradien d'Arnoux; **Sp**: ballenato
de Arnoux; **It**: berardio australe
• Significance of scientific name
Berardius = from *Berard*, the vessel that
transported passengers between France and
New Zealand, *arnuxi* = from Arnoux, the
name of a French surgeon
• Some data
Maximum length: 9.75 m;
Age reaches sexual maturity: 8 - 10 years;
Gestation period: 17 months;
Length at birth: 4 m;
Birth season: summer;
Length of dives: 60 min.;
Depth of dives: 1,000 m
• Distribution: Pelagic species, distributed in
southern oceans south of the Tropic of Capricorn
(23.5°S). Nothing is known about the abundance
of this species. Strandings and sightings near
New Zealand may indicate a concentration there.

BERARDIUS BAIRDI
Stejneger, 1883

• Common names: En: Baird's beaked
whale; **Fr**: baleine à bec de Baird; **Sp**: zifio
de Baird; **It**: berardio boreale
• Significance of scientific name
Berardius (see B. arnux), *bairdi* = from
Baird, American naturalist and secretary
of the Smithsonian Institution

• Some data
Maximum length: 12.8 m;
Length at birth: 4.5 m;
Maximum adult weight: 12 t;
Mating season: October - November;
Life span: 82 years;
Length of dives: 60 min.
Age reaches sexual maturity: 8 - 10 years;
Gestation period: 17 months
Depth of dives: 1,000 m (max. 2,400 m);

■ *The two species, even if living
in different areas, have the same
shape, livery and morphology.*

• Distribution: Pelagic species that lives in
the North Pacific from 34°N to the west,
to 24°N to the east. Still hunted in the
western North Pacific by the Japanese.

CEPHALORHYNCHUS COMMERSONI
Lacépède, 1804

Kerguelen Islands specimen

• **Common names: En**: Commerson's dolphin; **Fr**: dauphin de Commerson; **Sp**: tonina overa; **It**: cefalorinco di Commerson

• **Significance of scientific name**
Cephalorhynchus = from *cephalo*, Greek for head, *rhynchos* - nose or rostrum, *commersoni* = from Philibert Commerson, a 19th-century French physician and botanist who was the first to sight this species in 1767, near the Tierra del Fuego.

• **Some data**
Maximum length, in South America: 1.46 m females and 1.40 males;

Kerguelen Islands: 1.74 m females and 1.67 m males;
Maximum adult weight, South America: 66 kg;
Kerguelen Islands: 86 kg;
Life span: 18 years;
Age reaches sexual maturity: 5 - 8 years;
Gestation period: 11 - 12 months;
Length at birth: 0.55 - 0.65 m;
Weight at birth; 4.5 - 5.5 kg

• **Distribution:** Coastal species. Frequents the coasts of South America, from 53°S to 41°S to the Falkland Islands and the southern Shetland Islands. A second

population, probably genetically separate, lives near the Kerguelen Islands (at 50°S in the Indian Ocean). The two populations differ in size, colour, form and the cranium. It appears that a process of speciation is underway that will lead to the establishment of two distinct species. Moreno described this species for the first time in 1892, calling it *Lagenorhynchus floueri*. It was hunted to use as bait for fishing a species of crab known as centolla. It is documented that this species was whaled as long as 6000 years ago by the Fuegini Indians.

CEPHALORHYNCHUS EUTROPIA
Gray, 1846

• **Common names: En**: black dolphin; **Fr**: dauphin noir du Chili; **Sp**: delfin chileno; **It**: cefalorinco eutropia

• **Significance of scientific name**
Cephalorhynchus = from the Greek *cephalo*, head, *rhynchos* = nose or rostrum, *eutropia* = from *eu*, true or just, *tropis* = keel, due to the strongly carinate cranium

• **Some data**
Maximum length: 1.7 m;
Maximum adult weight: 63 kg;
Length at birth: 1 m

• **Distribution:** A coastal species, it lives along the coast of Chile from 33°S to 56°S. The black dolphin was hunted by the Fuegini Indians as early as 6000 years ago. Today its

meat is used as bait in fishing for the centolla and centollon crab. In 1846, Gray assigned this species to the genus Delphinus; in 1874 Dall correctly classified it under the genus Cephalorhynchus, although its name later underwent a number of changes. In all likelihood, the animal Lesson described in 1826 as *Delphinus lunatus* is *C. eutropia*.

CEPHALORHYNCHUS HEAVISIDII
Gray, 1828

- **Common names: En**: Heaviside's dolphin;
Fr: dauphin d'Heaviside; **Sp**: delfin de
Heaviside; **It**: cefalorinco di Heaviside
- **Significance of scientific name**
Cephalorhynchus = from the Greek *cephalo*,
head, *rhynchos* = nose or rostrum,
heavisidii = from Heaviside, captain of the
ship that first brought a specimen to
London in 1827

- **Some data**
Maximum length: 1.74 m;
Maximum adult weight; 70 - 80 kg;
Length at birth: 0.85 - 1 m;
Mating season: autumn
- **Distribution:** Lives along the coasts of
southern Africa. Its current distribution is
limited to the waters of the continental
shelf between the Cape of Good Hope and
the Kunene River, near the southern coasts

of West Africa. The first specimen was
described by Gray, who named the species
Delphinus heavisidii. Later, after analyzing the
cranium of the typical specimen, he classified
it under the genus Cephalorhynchus.
Synonyms for this species include:
Delphinus capensis Cuvier, 1829; *Delphinus
cephalorhynchus* Cuvier, 1836; *Delphinus
hastatus* Pucheran, 1856; and *Orca capensis*
van Beneden, 1873.

CEPHALORHYNCHUS HECTORI
van Beneden, 1881

- **Common names: En**: Hector's dolphin;
Fr: dauphin d'Hector; **Sp**: delfin de Hector;
It: cefalorinco di Hector
- **Significance of scientific name**
Cephalorhynchus = from the Greek *cephalo*,
head, *rhynchos* = nose or rostrum, *hectori* =
from Hector, a zoologist and curator of the
New Zealand Museum, who collected the
first specimen in 1869
- **Some data**
Maximum length: 1.67 m females

and 1.50 m males;
Maximum adult weight: 57.3 kg;
Age reaches sexual maturity; 7 - 9 years
females and 6 - 9 years males;
Length at birth: 0.6 - 0.7 m;
Weight at birth: 9.5 kg;
Birth season: spring
- **Distribution:** It lives along the coast
of New Zealand, where it normally
frequents shallow coastal waters.
The sharks *Notorhynchus cepedianus*

and *Prionacea glauca* are active predators
of this species.
Hector first described this dolphin
and gave it the name *Electra clancula.*
Van Beneden, who studied the same
specimen, understood that it was an
as yet unidentified species and called
it *Electra hectori.* Finally, Hector made
the correct classification, recognizing
it as a member of the genus
Cephalorhynchus.

DELPHINAPTERUS LEUCAS
Pallas, 1776

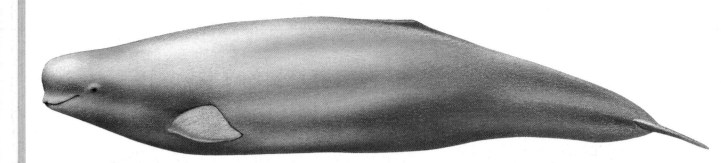

• **Common names: En**: white whale;
Fr: bélouga; **Sp**: beluga; **It**: beluga
• **Significance of scientific name**
Delphinos = dolphin, *a* = without
pteron = fin, *leukas* = white
• **Some data**
Maximum length: 4.1 m females
and 5.5 m males;
Maximum adult weight: 1.6 t;
Life span; 30 - 35 years;
Age reaches sexual maturity: 6 - 10 years;
Gestation period: 11 - 14 months;

Length at birth: 1.6 m;
Weight at birth: 79 kg;
Lactation: 20 - 24 months;
Mating season: spring - summer;
Length of dives: 15 min.;
Depth of dives; 647 m;
Maximum speed: 20 km/hr
• **Distribution**: Coastal species that lives
in the circumpolar Arctic.
• **Curious facts**: White whales are born
gray; they gradually grow lighter until
becoming white at about 5 years of age.

There has been much scientific debate on
what family this species belongs to. Some
writers have grouped it with the single
species genera Delphinapterus and Orcaella
in the Delphinapteridae family, based on
morphology studies of the tympanic
bones. In 1984, Barnes placed these two
species in the *Monodontidae* family.
Annual kills by Eskimo populations are
from 2% to 24% of each individual stock,
with the most kills along the Canadian
coasts (more than 3,000 animals a year).

DELPHINUS DELPHIS
Linnaeus, 1758

Delphinus capensis
Gray, 1928

• **Common names: En**: common dolphin;
Fr: dauphin commun; **Sp**: delfin comun;
It: delfino comune
• **Significance of scientific name**
Delphinus = Latin form of dolphin,
delphis = a Greek form of dolphin
• **Some data**
Maximum length: 2.4 m females
and 2.6 m males;
Maximum adult weight: 136 kg;
Life span: 20 years;
Age reaches sexual maturity: 6 - 7 years
females and 5 - 12 years males;
Gestation period: 10 months;

Length at birth: 0.80 - 0.85 m;
Lactation: 14 - 19 months;
Depth of dives: 280 m;
Mating season: spring - autumn;
Length of dives: 8 min.;
Maximum speed: 65 km/hr
• **Distribution**: Lives in all temperate and
tropical waters, preferring deep seas with
a surface temperature of about 10°C.
A population lives in the Black Sea and was
actively hunted until 1983; these individuals
are smaller than in other zones. The
population that lives in the western
Mediterranean has significantly decreased

and seems to have been replaced by the
striped dolphin. Numerous forms of this
species have been described, with great
variations in colour and morphological
characteristics: *D. longirostris, D. capensis, D.
rosiventris, D. baidii,* and *D. tropicalis*. At the
systematics level they are considered a single
species: *D. delphis*. Recent studies show that
D. capensis could be considered a species.
It is more coastal, but its distribution is
similar to *D. delphis*. The main differences
are a longer beak and more teeth. The form
that lives in the Indian Ocean, *D. tropicalis,*
could also be considered a third species.

FERESA ATTENUATA
Gray, 1875

• **Common names: En:** pygmy killer whale; **Fr:** orque pygmée; **Sp:** orca pigmea; **It:** feresa;
• **Significance of scientific name**
Feresa = common name for dolphin in French, *attenuata* = from the Latin *attenuatus*, thin, fine
• **Some data**
Maximum length: 2.43 m females and 2.87 m males;

Maximum adult weight: 225 kg;
Length at birth: 0.80 m;
Weight at birth: 9.37 kg
• **Distribution:** Despite scanty information, it is believed that this species is common in warm waters in seas all over the world.
The species gets its name from the research of John Gray of the British Museum. Gray examined two craniums,

classifying them as *F. intermedius* and *F. attenuata* respectively, in 1827 and 1874. Today only one widely distributed species is recognized.
Its similarities to other Odontocetes are not completely clear, in particular because the morphology of the accessory air sacs in the cranium and the tympanic bone is different. At present, it is classified as a member of the Delphinidae family.

GLOBICEPHALA MACRORHYNCHUS
Gray, 1846

• **Common names: En:** short-finned pilot whale; **Fr:** globicéphale tropical; **Sp:** calderón de aletas cortas; **It:** globicefalo di Gray
• **Significance of scientific name**
Globicephala = from the Latin, globe-shaped head, *macrorhynchus* = from the Latin, large beak
• **Some data**
Maximum length: 5.5 m females and 7.2 m males;

Maximum adult weight: 3.6 t;
Life span: females 63 years; males 46 years;
Age reaches sexual maturity: females 7 years, males 9 years;
Gestation period: 15 months;
Length at birth: 1.4 m;
Lactation: 12 months;
Birth interval for the same mother: 4 - 5 years;
Length of dives: 15 min.;
Depth of dives: 500 m

• **Distribution:**
Common in both neritic and pelagic areas in warm temperate, tropical and subtropical waters. We have information only on the population along the Japanese coast, which is comprised of two stocks, one northern and one southern. Annual kills by the Japanese, using harpoons or by stranding the animals on the beach, represent from 1% to 2% of the entire population.

GLOBICEPHALA MELAS
Traill, 1809

• **Common names: En**: long-finned pilot whale; **Fr**: globicéphale commun; **Sp**: calderón comun; **It**: globicefalo;

• **Significance of scientific name**
Globicephala = from the Latin, globe-shaped head, *melas* = from the Latin, black

• **Some data**
Maximum length: females 5.7 m, males 7.6 m;
Maximum adult weight: females 1 t, males 2 t;
Life span: 40 - 50 years;
Age reaches sexual maturity: females 6 - 10, males 15 -20;
Gestation period: 15 months;

Length at birth: 1.7 -1.8 m;
Weight at birth; 70 - 80 kg;
Lactation: 20 - 27 months;
Mating season; April and June;
Length of dives: 10 min.;
Depth of dives; 600 m;
Maximum speed; 35 km/hr

• **Distribution**: Pelagic species with antitropical distribution. Lives in the northern hemisphere above 30°N and in the southern hemisphere between the Tropic of Capricorn and the Antarctic convergence. In the Mediterranean, it is primarily concentrated in the Alboran Sea

southeast of Spain, a transition area between the Mediterranean and the Atlantic. The long-finned pilot whale is actively hunted in the Faer Øer Islands. Documentation of this practice dates back to 1584, but the activity itself is certainly much older.

GRAMPUS GRISEUS
G. Cuvier, 1812

• **Common names: En**: Risso's dolphin;
Fr: grampus; **Sp**: delfin de Risso; **It**: grampo

• **Significance of scientific name**
Grampus = an alteration of the Old French *graspeis*, in Latin *crassus piscis*, large fish, *griseus* = from the Latin, gray

• **Some data**

Total maximum length: 4.3 m;
Maximum adult weight: 500 kg;
Age reaches sexual maturity: 7 years;
Gestation period: 13 - 14 months;
Length at birth: 1.5 m;
Mating season: summer;
Maximum speed; 25 km/hr

• **Distribution:**
In the Atlantic, the northern limit of this species is Newfoundland and the Shetland Islands, while in the Pacific it is the Gulf of Alaska. To the south, it extends to Cape Horn, the Cape of Good Hope, Australia and New Zealand. No subspecies are known.

HYPEROODON AMPULLATUS
Forster, 1770

- **Common names: En**: northern bottlenose whale; **Fr**: hyperoodon boréal; **Sp**: ballena nariz de botella del norte; **It**: iperodonte boreale
- **Significance of scientific name**
Hyperoodon = from the Greek, *hyper* and *odon*, teeth in upper jaw, *ampullatus* = ampulla, due to the presence of papillae on the upper jaw erroneously identified as teeth

- **Some data**
Maximum length: females 8.7 m, males 9.80 m;
Life span: females 27 years, males 37 years;
Age reaches sexual maturity: females 11 years, males 7 - 11 years;
Gestation period: 12 months;
Length at birth: 3.5 m;
Lactation: 12 months;
Mating season: spring;
Length of dives: 70 min.;
- **Distribution:** It lives only in the North Atlantic

HYPEROODON PLANIFRONS
Flower, 1882

- **Common names: En**: southern bottlenose whale; **Fr**: hyperoodon austral; **Sp**: ballena nariz de botella del sur; **It**: iperodonte australe
- **Significance of scientific name**
Hyperoodon = from the Greek *hyper* and *odon*, teeth in upper jaw, *planifrons* = from the Latin, flat front
- **Some data**
Maximum length: females 7.8 m; males 7.2 m;
Life span: 50 years;
Age reaches sexual maturity: females 12 years; males 20 years;
Length at birth: 2 m

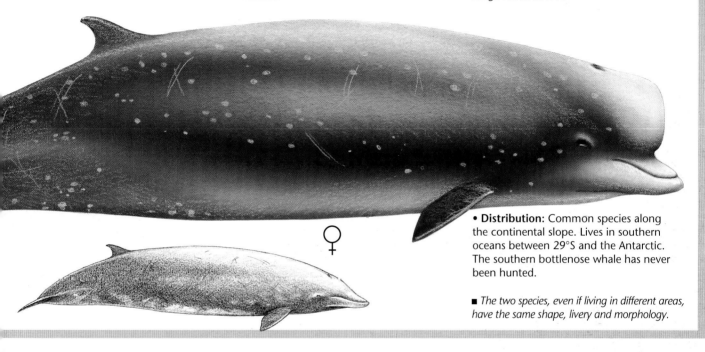

♀

- **Distribution:** Common species along the continental slope. Lives in southern oceans between 29°S and the Antarctic. The southern bottlenose whale has never been hunted.

■ *The two species, even if living in different areas, have the same shape, livery and morphology.*

INIA GEOFFRENSIS
de Blainville, 1817

- **Common names: En**: boto; **Fr** : inia; **Sp**: bufeo; **It**: inia
- **Significance of scientific name**
Inia = the name used for these dolphins by the Guarayo Indios along the San Miguel River in Bolivia, *geoffrensis* = from Geoffrey St. Hilaire, a naturalist who collected specimens for Napoleon
- **Some data**
Maximum length: females 2.3 m; males 2.8 m;

Maximum adult weight: females 100 kg; males 160 kg;
Life span: 30 years;
Gestation period: 10 - 11 months;
Length at birth: 0.80 m;
Weight at birth: 7 - 8 kg;
Lactation: 1 year;
Maximum speed: 3.2 km/hr
- **Distribution:** River species. There are no estimates on the size of the boto's population. It lives in the Amazon and

Orinoco rivers. In 1817 de Blainville described this species as *Delphinus geoffrensis*. Some authors recognize three subspecies: *I.g. boliviensis* (Bolivian population), *I.g. geoffrensis* (Amazon population) and *I.g. humboldtiana* (Orinoco population). Its place in the Platanistidae family is also controversial. In his 1991 book *Dolphins, Porpoises and Whales of the World*, Klinowska includes it in a separate family, Iniidae.

KOGIA BREVICEPS
de Blainville, 1838

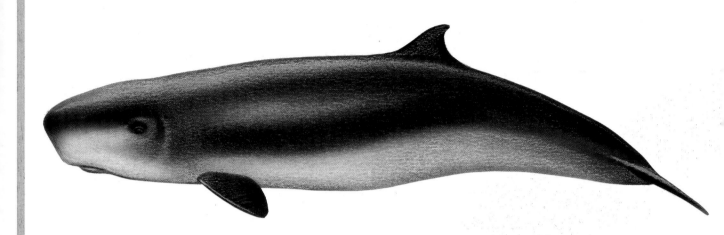

- **Common names: En:** pygmy sperm whale; **Fr:** cachalot pygmée; **Sp:** cachalote pigmeo; **It:** cogia di Blainville
- **Significance of scientific name**
Kogia = a latinized form of *codger* (see *K. simus*), *breviceps* = short, small
- **Some data**
Maximum length: 3.40 m;
Adult weight: 400 kg;
Gestation period: 9 - 11 months;
Length at birth: 1 - 1.20 m;
Lactation: 12 months;
Mating season: summer;
Depth of dives: 200 m
- **Distribution:** Lives in tropical, subtropical and temperate seas, although we still know little of this species. The scanty knowledge we have comes almost exclusively from observations of stranded animals. In 1993, 51 individuals were accidentally captured, caught in the floating Japanese and Taiwanese nets operating in the North Pacific.

KOGIA SIMUS
Owen, 1866

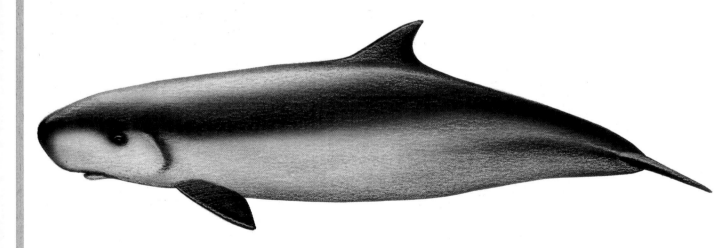

- **Common names: En:** dwarf sperm whale; **Fr:** cachalot nain; **Sp:** cachalote enano; **It:** cogia di Owen;
- **Significance of scientific name**
Kogia = a latinized form of the word codger (as in "old codger"); *Kogia* may also refer to the name of a Turk, Cogia Effendi, who observed whales in the Mediterranean; *simus* = with a short snout
- **Some data**
Maximum length: 2.74 m;
Maximum adult weight: 272 kg;
Gestation period: 9 months;
Length at birth: 1 m;
Mating season: summer;
Depth of dives: 300 m
- **Distribution:** The little information we have seems to indicate that the two species of *Kogia* have similar behaviours and distribution. It nevertheless appears to be more common that was formerly thought. The English anatomist Owen first described this species in 1866, but it was not recognized as a separate species until a century later. In the 1993 stranding of *Kogia breviceps* in the North Pacific, 17 individuals of this species were also caught.

LAGENODELPHIS HOSEI
Fraser, 1956

• **Common names: En**: Fraser's dolphin;
Fr: dauphin de Fraser; **Sp**: delfin de Fraser;
It: lagenodelfino
• **Significance of scientific name**
Lagenos = from the Greek, bottle, *delphinus*
= dolphin, *hosei* = from C. Hose, who
collected the first specimen
• **Some data**
Maximum length 2.7 m;

Maximum adult weight: 200 kg;
Age reaches sexual maturity: females
8 years, males 7 years;
Length at birth: 1 m;
Depth of dives: 250 m
• **Distribution**: Has a pantropical distribution
between 40°N and 40°S. Common in the
Philippine Sea, and has also been sighted in
the tropical Pacific along the equator. This

species is hunted and eaten throughout
the Indo-Pacific. F. C. Fraser, researcher of
the British Museum, described the species
in 1956, basing his study on a skeleton
collected in the late 19th century on a beach
at Sarawak in Borneo. The genus name
comes from the fact that the cranium has
characteristics that reflect both
Lagenorhynchus and *Delphinus* genera.

LAGENORHYNCHUS ACUTUS
Gray, 1828

• **Common names: En**: Atlantic white-sided
dolphin; **Fr**: dauphin à flancs blancs de
l'atlantique; **Sp**: delfin de flancos blancos;
It: lagenorinco acuto
• **Significance of scientific name**
Lagenorhynchus = from the Greek *lagenos* =
bottle, *rhynchus* = snout, nose, *acutus* =
from the Latin, pointed
• **Some data**
Maximum length: females 2.5 m

and males 2.8 m;
Maximum adult weight: 235 kg;
Life span: females 27 years, males 22 years;
Age reaches sexual maturity: 6 - 12 years
Gestation period: 10 - 12 months;
Length at birth: 1.1 - 1.2 m;
Lactation: 18 months;
Mating season: summer
• **Distribution**: Pelagic species in the
northwestern Atlantic, where the surface

water temperature is 9 - 15°C, between
the warm Gulf Stream and the cold coastal
waters influenced by the Labrador Current.
It is considered locally abundant. Migrates
seasonally, concentrating on the
continental slope.
There is no information on the size of the
population. Small numbers are
occasionally caught on the Faer Øer
Islands and in Greenland.

LAGENORHYNCHUS ALBIROSTRIS
Gray, 1846

• **Common names: En**: white-beaked dolphin; **Fr**: dauphin à bec blanc; **Sp**: delfin de hocico blanco; **It**: lagenorinco rostrobianco
• **Significance of scientific name**
Lagenorhynchus = from the Greek *lagenos* = bottle, *rhyncus* = snout, nose, *albirostris* = from the Latin, white rostrum

• **Some data**
Maximum length: females 3.05 m, males 3.15 m;
Length at birth: 1.2 - 1.6 m;
Mating season: summer;
Length of dives: 6 min.;
Depth of dives: 215 m

• **Distribution**: Broadly distributed in the northern and subarctic area of the North Atlantic. Abundant in the Norwegian Sea, the North Sea, the southwestern Barents Sea, around Labrador, along the Strait of Denmark and south of the Davis Strait. A few dozen are occasionally caught for food in the Faer Øer Islands and Greenland.

LAGENORHYNCHUS AUSTRALIS
Peale, 1848

• **Common names: En**: Peale's dolphin; **Fr**: dauphin de Peale; **Sp**: delfin austral; **It**: lagenorinco australe
• **Significance of scientific name**
Lagenorhynchus = from the Greek *lagenos* = bottle, *rhynchus* = snout, nose, *australis* = southern
• **Some data**
Maximum length: 2.16 m;
Maximum adult weight: 115 kg;

Length at birth: 1 m;
Mating season: autumn
• **Distribution:**
It has a rather limited distribution. It prefers the waters of the continental shelf and slope of fjords, straits and inlets in southern South America, from Chile to Tierra del Fuego, in particular the Beagle Channel and Argentina. The naturalist Peale first described this species, giving it

the name *Phocoena australis* based on a specimen harpooned on February 12, 1839 during the United States Exploring Expedition. No subspecies are known. There are no estimates on size of population, but several thousand individuals are killed each year in Chile and used as bait for centolla crabs. This species is used in a similar manner in Argentina.

LAGENORHYNCHUS CRUCIGER
Quoy and Gaimard, 1824

- **Common names: En**: hourglass dolphin;
Fr: dauphin crucigère; **Sp**: delfin cruzado;
It: lagenorinco dalla croce
- **Significance of scientific name**
Lagenorhynchus = from the Greek *lagenos* =
bottle, *rhyncus* = snout, nose, *cruciger* =
from the Latin *crucis* and *gero* = carrying a
cross, which refers to the marking in the
form of a cross visible on its flanks where
two white areas intersect
- **Some data**
Maximum length: females 1.83 m,
males 1.63 m;
Length at birth: 1 m

- **Distribution**: Pelagic species. Lives in the
circumpolar zone at high latitudes in
southern oceans. Quoy and Gaimard first
described this species, naming it *Delphinus
cruciger*. The population seems to be in
satisfactory condition.

LAGENORHYNCHUS OBLIQUIDENS
Gill, 1865

- **Common names: En**: Pacific white-sided
dolphin; **Fr**: dauphin à flancs blancs du
Pacifique; **Sp**: delfin de costados blancos
del Pacifico; **It**: lagenorinco dai denti obliqui
- **Significance of scientific name**
Lagenorhynchus = from the Greek *lagenos*
= bottle, *rhynchus* = snout, nose;
obliquidens = from the Latin *obliquus* and
dens = oblique tooth
- **Some data**
Maximum length: 2.5 m;
Maximum adult weight: 180 kg;
Life span: 46 years;
Gestation period: 10 -12 months;
Length at birth: 0.80 m;
Mating season: autumn

- **Distribution**: Pelagic species.
The population is divided into two
stocks, one in the northwestern Pacific
and one in the northeastern Pacific,
separated by an area with a low
density population south of the Aleutian
Islands.

LAGENORHYNCHUS OBSCURUS
Gray, 1828

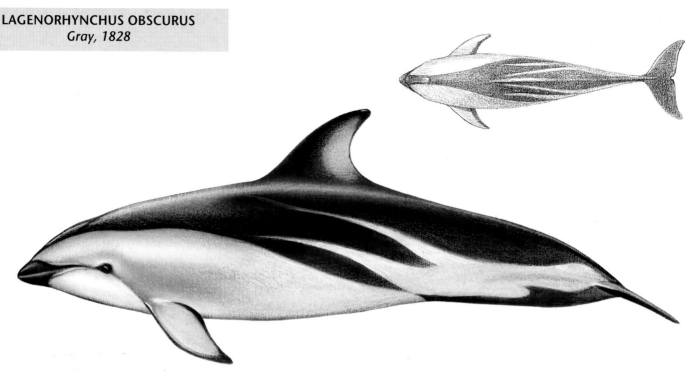

- **Common names: En:** dusky dolphin; **Fr:** dauphin sombre; **Sp:** delfin obscuro; **It:** lagenorinco scuro
- **Significance of scientific name**
Lagenorhynchus = from the Greek *lagenos* = bottle, and *rhyncus* = snout, nose, *obscurus* = from the Latin, dark
- **Some data**
Maximum length: 2.1 m;

Maximum adult weight: 80 kg ;
Gestation period: 11 months;
Length at birth: 0.5 - 0.7 m;
Weight at birth: 3.7 kg;
Lactation: 18 months;
Mating season: November - February
- **Distribution:** Coastal species in the waters of New Zealand, South America and southern Africa. The distribution

of this species has areas of discontinuity, and there are no estimates on the size of the population. The dusky dolphin is hunted in the waters of Peru. Probably several thousand are caught in stand nets each year for food purposes. Gray described this species based on a cranium from the Cape of Good Hope, and called it *Delphinus obscurus*.

LIPOTES VEXILLIFER
Miller, 1918

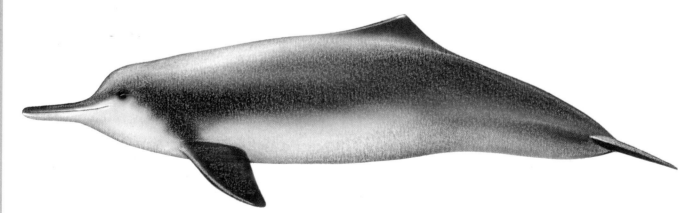

- **Common names: En:** baiji; **Fr:** dauphin fluvitil de Chine; **Sp:** platanista del Yangtze; **It:** lipote
- **Significance of scientific name**
Lipotes = from *leipo*, a Greek name that means "left behind," in reference to the limited distribution of this species, *vexillifer* = from the Latin *vexillum* and *fer*, carry the flag
- **Some data**
Maximum length: females 2.53 m, males 2.16 m;
Maximum adult weight: 160 kg;
Length at birth: 0.95 m;

Weight at birth: 9.5 kg;
Maximum speed: 1.2 m/sec
- **Distribution:** River species. The baiji lives only in China, along the Yangtze River, concentrated primarily in the intermediate and lower waterway. The dolphins also enter Boyanghu and Dungtinghu lakes during the rainy season when the water level is high. The population is in danger for a number of reasons.
Heavy riverfishing limits the availability of food; dams have changed the flood plains, which are important areas for the reproduction of the fish on which the baiji

feeds. Attempts are being made to raise and breed them in captivity.
A public awareness campaign is also underway with people living along the Yangtze River. The Chinese knew of and mentioned this species as early as 2000 years ago, calling it *Baiji*, which means white. Its systematic position has changed a number of times. At first it was placed in a different family, Lipotidae, due to skeletal differences from the boto and the river dolphin. More accurate analyses include it with these species in the Platanistidae family.

LISSODELPHIS BOREALIS
Peale, 1848

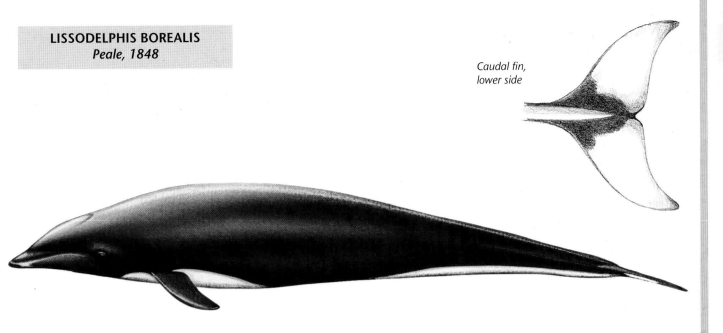

Caudal fin,
lower side

- **Common names: En**: northern right whale dolphin; **Fr**: dauphin à dos lisse boréal; **Sp**: delfin liso del norte; **It**: lissodelfino boreale
- **Significance of scientific name**
Lissodelphis = from *lisso*, Greek for smooth, because it has no dorsal fin; *delphis* = dolphin, *borealis* = northern
- **Some data**
Maximum length: females 2.3 m, males 3.1 m;

Maximum adult weight: 115 kg;
Age reaches sexual maturity: females 12 years, males 11 years;
Length at birth: 0.80 - 1 m;
Length of dives: 6.25 min.;
Depth of dives: 200 m;
Maximum speed: 34 km/hr
- **Distribution**: This species frequents the deep waters of the continental shelf of the North Pacific Ocean, east between 30°N and 50°N, and west between 35°N

and 51°N. A pelagic species, it may approach the coast near underwater canyons. Peale, who described the first specimen, caught along the northwest coast of North America, called it *Delphinapterus borealis*.
Based on information from the Scientific Commission, the International Whaling Commission has decided to revise the systematics of the genus Lissodelphis by 1999.

LISSODELPHIS PERONI
Lacépède, 1804

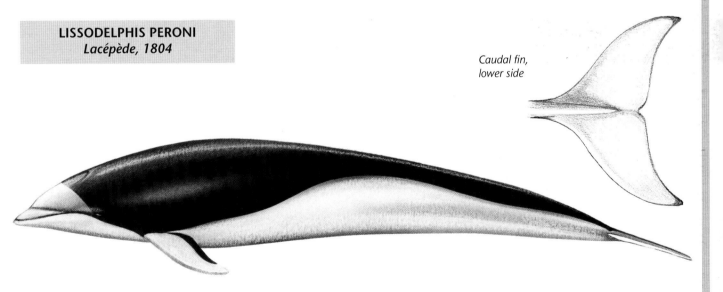

Caudal fin,
lower side

- **Common names: En**: southern right whale dolphin; **Fr**: dauphin aptère austral; **Sp**: delfin liso austral; **It**: lissodelfino australe
- **Significance of scientific name**
Lissodelphis = from *lisso*, which in Greek means smooth, *delphis* = dolphin; *peroni* = from F. Peron, a French naturalist who lived between the 18th and 19th centuries
- **Some data**
Maximum length: 2.97 m;
Maximum adult weight: 116 kg;

Length at birth: 1 m;
Length of dives: 6.5 min.;
Depth of dives: 200 m;
Maximum speed: 22 km/hr
- **Distribution**: Unlike the northern species, the southern right whale dolphin is distributed along the entire temperate region of the southern hemisphere, where the temperature varies from 1° to 20°C. Schools of over 1,000 individuals are known, but there are no estimates for the entire

population. Maximum concentrations are near the Antarctic convergence, while a more northerly sighting was made at about 19°S off the coast of Chile. It is hunted in Peru and Chile to make bait for fishing for *centolla* crabs or for food. Lacépède first named this species *Delphinus peroni*. Based on information from the Scientific Commission, the IWC has decided to revise the systematics of the genus Lissodelphis by 1999.

The Beaked Whales (Mesoplodon)

All species of beaked whales are pelagic and little is known about them. There is no information on population size.
• **Significance of scientific name**
Mesos, hopla, odon = three Greek words that mean "tooth in middle of jaw"

MESOPLODON BAHAMONDI
Mead and van Waerebeek, 1995

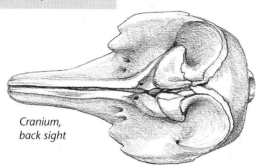

Cranium, back sight

Cranium, lateral sight

A new species of beaked whale was described in 1995 on the basis of a cranium found on Robinson Crusoe Island in the Juan Fernández archipelago in Chile. The order of the Mesoplodon genus is defined by the shape and arrangement of the teeth in adult males and it was on the basis of these characteristics that it was possible to confirm that this species is different from the morphologically similar species called Andrew's beaked whale - *Mesoplodon bowdoni*. The possible relationship between this new species of Zifide and an unidentified species *(Mesoplodon sp.)* sighted in the Eastern tropical Pacific and described by the researchers Pitman, Aguayo and Urban in 1987 is the subject of scientific debate.

MESOPLODON BIDENS
Sowerby, 1804

Shape of the tooth

• **Common names: En**: Sowerby's beaked whale; **Fr**: baleine à bec de Sowerby; **Sp**: zifio de Sowerby; **It**: mesoplodonte di Sowerby

• **Some data**
Maximum length: 5 m;
Length at birth: 2.4 m;
Weight at birth: 185 kg;
Mating season: late winter and spring

• **Distribution:** Lives in the North Atlantic. Its presence in the Mediterranean is controversial.

MESOPLODON BOWDOINI
Andrews, 1908

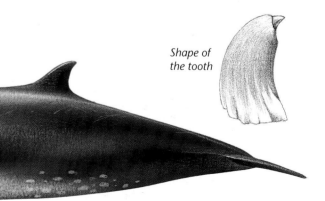

Shape of the tooth

• **Common names: En**: Andrews' beaked whale; **Fr**: baleine à bec de Bowdoin; **Sp**: zifio de Andrews; **It**: mesoplodonte di Bowdoin

• **Some data**
Maximum length: 4.7 m;
Length at birth: 2 m

• **Distribution:** All that is known about this species is through strandings along the southern coast of Australia, New Zealand and the Kerguelen Islands.

MESOPLODON CARLHUBBSI
Moore, 1963

Shape of the tooth

• **Common names: En**: Hubbs' beaked whale; **Fr**: baleine à bec de Hubbs; **Sp**: zifio de Hubbs; **It**: mesoplodonte di Hubbs

• **Some data**
Maximum length: 5.3 m;
Maximum adult weight; 1.4 t;
Length at birth: 2.5 m

• **Distribution:**
Its distribution is limited to the North Pacific, To the east it is present between 33°N and 51°N, while to the west sightings have been only in Japan (38°N).

MESOPLODON DENSIROSTRIS
de Blainville, 1817

Shape of the tooth

• **Common names: En**: Blainville's beaked whale; **Fr**: baleine à bec de Blainville; **Sp**: zifio de Blainville; **It**: mesoplodonte di Blainville

• **Some data**
Maximum length: females 4.7 m, males 5.8 m;
Maximum adult weight: 1 t;
Length at birth; 2 - 2.6 m;
Weight at birth: 60 kg

• **Distribution:** The species is present in temperate and tropical waters of the Caribbean Sea, the Gulf of Mexico and the Bahamas.

MESOPLODON EUROPAEUS
Gervais, 1855

Shape of the tooth

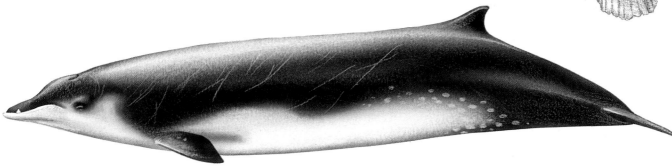

• **Common names: En**: Gervais' beaked whale; **Fr**: baleine à bec de Gervais; **Sp**: zifio de Gervais; **It**: mesoplodonte di Gervais

• **Some data**
Maximum length: females 5.2 m, males 4.5 m;
Maximum adult weight: 1.2 t;
Life span: 48 years;

Length at birth: 2.1 m;
Weight at birth: 49 kg
• **Distribution:** Inhabits the tropical and warm temperate waters of the Atlantic.

MESOPLODON GINKGODENS
Nishiwaki and Kamiya, 1958

Shape of the tooth

- **Common names: En**: ginkgo-toothed beaked whale; **Fr**: baleine à bec de Nishiwaki; **Sp**: zifio japonés; **It**: mesoplodonte di Nishiwaki

- **Some data**
Maximum length: 4.9 m;
Length at birth: 2 - 2.5 m

- **Distribution**: Only 13 stranded animals have been found, 10 in the North Pacific, 2 in the Indian Ocean and 1 in the South Pacific.

MESOPLODON GRAYI
Haast, 1876

Shape of the tooth

- **Common names: En**: Gray's beaked whale; **Fr**: baleine à bec de Gray; **Sp**: Zifio de Gray; **It**: mesoplodonte di Gray
- **Some data**
Maximum length: 5.33 m females

and 5.64 m males;
Maximum adult weight: 1 t;
Length at birth: 2 - 2.5 m
- **Distribution**: The species has been sighted along the coast of New Zealand,

Australia, South Africa, Argentina and Chile. The only documentation in the northern hemisphere is an individual stranded in the Netherlands in 1927.

MESOPLODON HECTORI
Gray, 1871

Shape of the tooth

- **Common names: En**: Hector's beaked whale; **Fr**: baleine à bec d' Hector; **Sp**: zifio de Hector; **It**: mesoplodonte di Hector

- **Some data**
Maximum length: 4.4 m;
Length at birth; 2.1 m

- **Distribution**: The few sightings have been in the southern hemisphere, in Chile, Argentina, New Zealand and South Africa.

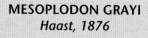

Shape of
the tooth

MESOPLODON LAYARDI
Gray, 1865

• **Common names: En**: strap-toothed whale; **Fr**: baleine à bec de Layard; **Sp**: zifio de Layard; **It**: mesoplodonte di Layard

• **Some data**
Maximum length: females 6.2 m, males 5.9 m;
Maximum adult weight: 1.4 t;
Length at birth: 3 m;
Mating season; spring and early summer

• **Distribution:** This is a cold temperate water species which has been sighted in the Indian and Pacific Oceans.

MESOPLODON MIRUS
True, 1913

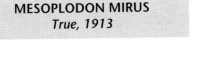

Shape of
the tooth

• **Common names: En**: True's beaked whale; **Fr**: baleine à bec de True; **Sp**: zifio de True; **It**: mesoplodonte di True
• **Some data**
Maximum length: 5 m;

Maximum adult weight: 1.4 t;
Length at birth: 2,5 m;
Weight at birth: 136 kg
• **Distribution:** In the North Atlantic, its territory extends from Nova Scotia to the

Bahamas. To the east it is present in the Hebrides to southern France. In the southern hemisphere there have been strandings in South Africa and Australia.

MESOPLODON PACIFICUS
Longman, 1926

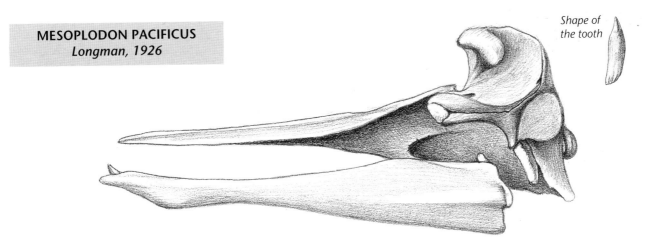

Shape of
the tooth

• **Common names: En**: Longman's beaked whale; **Fr**: baleine à bec de Longman; **Sp**: zifio de Longman; **It**: mesoplodonte di Longman

• **Some data**
Maximum length: 6 m
• **Distribution:** A complete animal has

never been identified. Only two craniums have been found, one in Somalia and the other in Queensland, Australia.

MESOPLODON PERUVIANUS
Reyes, Mead and Waerebeek, 1991

Shape of the tooth

• **Common names: En**: pygmy beaked whale; **Fr**: baleine à bec pygmée; **Sp**: ballena picuda; **It**: mesoplodonte peruviano
• **Some data**
Maximum length: 3.7 m;

Length at birth: 1.6 m
• **Distribution**: It is only known through 10 individual strandings and a few sightings in Peru beyond 8°S, in the eastern tropical Pacific. Recently there

have been two strandings near La Paz, in the Bay of California, Mexico. Identifiable by a small dorsal fin different from those of other species in the Mesoplodon genus.

MESOPLODON SP.

• **Common names: En**: mesoplodon; **Fr**: mesoplodon; **Sp**: mesoplodon; **It**: mesoplodonte

• **Some data**
Maximum length: 5.5 m
• **Distribution**: This species has been

noted in the eastern tropical Pacific and was described by the researchers Pitman, Aguayo and Urban in 1987.

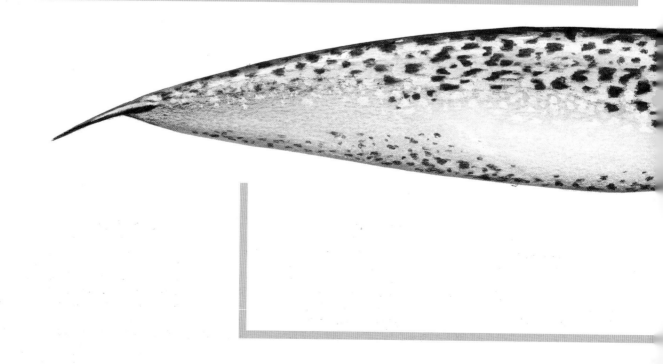

MESOPLODON STEJNEGERI
True, 1885

Shape of the tooth

- **Common names: En**: Stejneger's beaked whale; **Fr**: baleine à bec de Stejneger; **Sp**: zifio de Stejneger; **It**: mesoplodonte di Stejneger

- **Some data**
Maximum length: 5.25 m;
Length at birth: 2.5 m;
Depth of dives: 730 - 1560 m

- **Distribution**: Its territory extends through the North Pacific, with most sightings along the Alaska coast.

MONODON MONOCEROS
Linnaeus, 1758

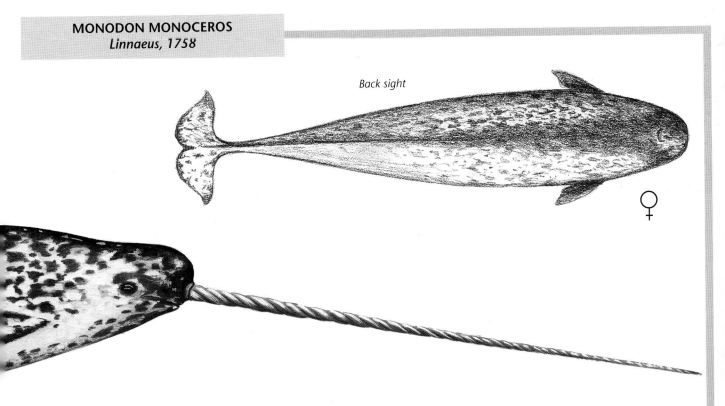

Back sight

♀

- **Common names: En**: narwhal; **Fr**: narval; **Sp**: narval; **It**: narvalo;
- **Significance of scientific name**
Mono = one, *odon* = tooth and *ceros* = horn
- **Some data**
Maximum length: females 4.2 m, males 4.7 m;
Maximum adult weight: females 900 kg,

males 1,600 kg;
Life span: 50 years;
Age reaches sexual maturity; females 5 - 8 years, males 11 - 13 years;
Gestation period; 15 months;
Length at birth: 1.6 m;
Weight at birth: 80 kg;
Lactation: 20 months;

Mating season: March - May;
Length of dives: 20 min.;
Depth of dives: 1,000 m
- **Distribution**: Coastal species with northern circumpolar distribution. It is rarely seen below 60°N. Arctic peoples kill about a thousand animals a year for their meat and ivory.

NEOPHOCAENA PHOCAENOIDES
G. Cuvier, 1829

• **Common names: En**: finless porpoise;
Fr: marsouin aptère; **Sp**: marsopa lisa or
sin aleta; **It**: neofocena
• **Significance of scientific name**
Neophocaena phocaenoides comes from the
Greek, "new species of porpoise similar to
Phocoena"
• **Some data**
Maximum length: 1.9 m;
Gestation period; 10 - 11 months;
Length at birth: 0.7 - 0.8 m;
Lactation: 6 - 15 months;
Mating season: spring
• **Distribution:** Coastal and river species.
Lives in the waters of Japan, Malaysia,
China, Pakistan and India.

Cuvier described this species in 1829
and called it *Delphinus phocaenoides*.
Later, Gray (1846) placed it in a new
genus, *Neomeris*, while Palmer (1899)
placed it in *Neophocaena*. Pilleri and
Gihr (1971) proposed the existence of
two species, one with a more eastern
distribution (China, Korea and Japan),
and called it *Neomeris asiaeorientalis*.
In a later revision, the same authors
changed the name to *Neophocaena
asiaeorientalis* and distinguished the
present form in Japan by the name
Neophocaena sunameri. At present it
is held that there is only one species,
N. phocaenoides.

ORCAELLA BREVIROSTRIS
Gray, 1866

• **Common names: En**: irrawaddy dolphin;
Fr: orcelle; **Sp**: delfin del Irawaddy; **It**: orcella
• **Significance of scientific name**
Orcaella = orca, cetacean, *brevirostris* =
globular, short head
• **Some data**
Maximum length: 2.75 m;
Maximum adult weight: 150 kg;
Life span: 30 years;
Age reaches sexual maturity: 4 - 6 years;
Gestation period: 14 months;
Length at birth: 1 m;

Weight at birth: 12.5 kg;
Mating season: spring and early summer;
Length of dives: 12 min.;
Maximum speed: 20-25 km/hr
• **Distribution:** Coastal and river species.
It is believed they are relatively common,
especially in northern Australia and in the
lower Irrawaddy River. In Australia, several
dozen are caught in shark nets each year.
• **Curious facts:** Vietnamese and Khmer
fishermen consider the irrawaddy dolphin
a sacred animal, and if accidentally caught,

they will free it. In the Mekong area,
the bodies of these animals are cremated
with religious ceremonies. John Gray of
the British Museum was the first to classify
this species. His systematics is still being
debated, and not all authors agree with
his attribution to the Monodontidae
family. The genus name currently in
use was attributed by Gray, who based
it on a cranium which Owen had
previously described as *Phocoena
brevirostris* in 1869.

♀

• **Common names: En**: killer whale; **Fr**: orque; **Sp**: orca; **It**: orca

• **Significance of scientific name**
Orcinus = from orca, and *orca* = a very ferocious animal with a barrel-shaped body

• **Some data**
Maximum length: females 8.5 m, males 9.8 m;
Maximum weight: females 7.5 t; males 10 t;
Life span: 35 - 50 years;
Age reaches sexual maturity: females 6 - 10 years, males 12 - 16 years;
Gestation period: 12 - 16 months;
Length at birth: 2 - 2.5 m;

Weight at birth: 180 kg;
Lactation: 15 months;
Depth of dives: 1,000 m;
Mating season: spring, early summer;
Length of dives: 20 min.;
Maximum speed: 55 km/hr

• **Distribution**: Common in all oceans. In his first description, Linnaeus called this species *Delphinus orca*. *Orcinus* was introduced by Fitzinger in 1860. In 1880, van Beneden and Gervais used the term *Orca gladiator*. In later revisions, it was placed in the genus Grampus and the name *Grampus rectipinna* was proposed for

specimens with a more developed fin. At present only one species is recognized, *Orcinus orca*, which is widely distributed. It is both coastal and pelagic, depending on the area of distribution.

• **Curious facts:** On October 12, 1958, a male 6 meters long was identified moving at the speed of 55 kilometers an hour. Dall's porpoises can reach the same speed for brief distances. Since 1988, the Vancouver aquarium has featured the radio show "Orca" on 88.5 FM, which broadcasts the voices of these cetaceans.

PEPONOCEPHALA ELECTRA
Gray, 1846

• **Common names:**
En: melon-headed whale;
Fr: péponocéphale; **Sp**: calderón
pequeño; **It**: peponocefalo
• **Significance of scientific name**
Peponocephala = melon-headed; *electra* =
from Electra, a nymph in Greek mythology

• **Some data**
Maximum length: 2.75 m;
Maximum adult weight: 275 kg;
Life span: 47 years;
Age reaches sexual maturity: 14 years;
Gestation period: 1 year;
Length at birth: 1 m;
Mating season: July - August

• **Distribution:** Few living or stranded
animals have been sighted, but it is believed
they live in temperate waters of all oceans.
Gray initially called this species
Lagenorhynchus electra. Other synonyms are
Lagenorhynchus asia (Gray, 1846); *Delphinus
pectoralis* (Peale, 1848); *Lagenorhynchus
pectoralis* (Cassin, 1858); *Delphinus fusiformis*
(Owen, 1866); *Electra asia* (Gray, 1868) and
Electra obtusa (Gray, 1868).

PHOCOENA PHOCOENA
Linnaeus, 1758

• **Common names: En**: harbour
porpoise; **Fr**: marsouin commun;
Sp: marsopa comun; **It**: focena
• **Significance of scientific name**
Phocoena = similar to a seal or small
cetacean
• **Some data**
Maximum length: 2 m;
Maximum adult weight: 70 kg;
Life span: 15 years;

Age reaches sexual maturity: 5 - 6 years;
Gestation period: 10 - 11 months;
Length at birth: 0.7 - 0.9 m;
Lactation: 8 months;
Birth interval for the same mother: 1year;
Mating season: May and September
• **Distribution:** Coastal species.
Prefers estuaries and inlets. Lives in the
North Pacific, from Japan to central
California. In all areas, many individuals

are caught in fishing nets. An annual
mortality rate of 3% to 10% has been
calculated. The harbour porpoise is
hunted and eaten in Greenland.
There are some indications of it in the
western Mediterranean basin. At first,
Linnaeus called this species *Delphinus
phocoena*. Later, in 1817, Cuvier classified
it under the genus Phocoena.
No subspecies are known.

PHOCOENA SINUS
Norris and McFarland, 1958

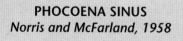

• **Common names: En**: Vaquita; **Fr**:
Marsouin du Golfe de Californie; **Sp**:
Vaquita; **It**: focena del Golfo della California
• **Significance of scientific name**
Phocoena = from the Greek, small
cetacean, *sinus* = from the Latin, inlet, bay

• **Some data**
Maximum length: females 1.50 m;
males 1.45 m
• **Distribution:** Coastal species. A few
hundred individuals live in the Gulf of
California. It is accidentally caught (30-40
individuals a year) in shark nets and trawl

nets for shrimp. Fishermen have given it
the name vaquita ("little cow").
Due to its restricted area of distribution,
the vaquita is probably the most
endangered of all cetaceans.
Described for the first time in 1958, it lives
only in the Gulf of California.

PHOCOENA SPINIPINNIS
Burmeister, 1865

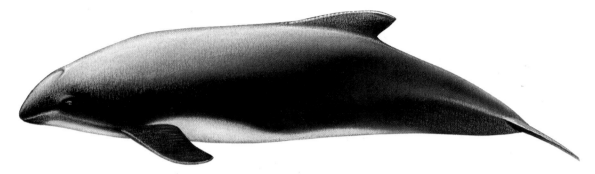

• **Common names: En:** Burmeister's porpoise; **Fr:** marsouin de Burmeister; **Sp:** marsopa espinosa; **It:** focena spinipinne
• **Significance of scientific name**
Phocoena = from the Greek, small dolphin, *spinipinnis* = from the Latin, fin with spines

• **Some data**
Maximum length: 1.85 m;
Maximum adult weight: 85 kg;
Length at birth; 0.8 - 0.9 m
• **Distribution:** Coastal species. The Burmeister's porpoise lives along the Atlantic and Pacific coasts of South America, and is more abundant in the

western area of its distribution. Like *Cephalorhynchus*, its meat is used as bait for *centolla* crabs. In Peru it is caught for food. Burmeister, the director of the Museum of Natural History in Buenos Aires, gave it the species name *spinipinnis* due to the presence of many small horny spines (tubercles) on the dorsal fin.

PHOCOENOIDES DALLI
True, 1885

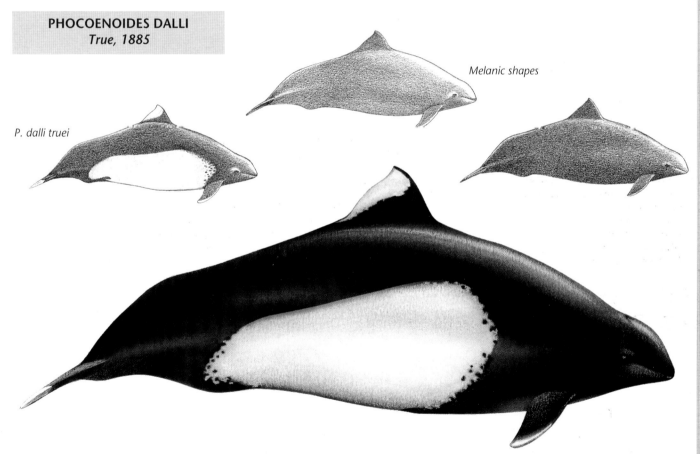

P. dalli truei

Melanic shapes

• **Common names: En:** Dall's porpoise; **Fr:** marsouin de Dall; **Sp:** marsopa de Dall; **It:** focenoide
• **Significance of scientific name**
Phocoena = from the Greek, small dolphin; *oides* = from the Greek *eides*, similar to; *dalli* = from W. H. Dall, an eminent American zoologist
• **Some data**
Maximum length: 2.4 m;
Maximum adult weight: 200 kg;

Life span: 10 years;
Age reaches sexual maturity: females 3 - 4 years; males 6 years;
Gestation period: 11.5 months;
Length at birth: 1 m;
Maximum speed: 55 km/hr
• **Distribution:** A pelagic species, it is present only in the North Pacific. Its territory extends from the waters of Japan, across the North Pacific, to the Bering Sea, and along the western coast of North

America to California. The Dall's porpoise is still caught for food by Japanese fishermen. In 1885, at the request of his colleague Dall, True, the director of the National Museum's Biology Institute in the United States, classified this species as *Phocoena dalli*. No subspecies are known, but two morphologically distinguishable forms have been described, the oceanic Dall's porpoise (*P. d. dalli*), and the coastal True's porpoise (*P. d. truei*).

PHYSETER CATODON
Linnaeus, 1758

- **Common names: En**: sperm whale; **Fr**: cachalot; **Sp**: cachalote; **It**: capodoglio
- **Significance of scientific name**
Physeter = blow, *catodon* = large teeth
- **Some data**
Maximum length: 12.5 m females; 18.3 m males;
Maximum adult weight: 57 t males; 24 t females;
Life span: 60 - 70 years;
Age reaches sexual maturity: 7 - 13 years

females, 18 - 21 years males;
Gestation period: 14 - 15 months;
Length at birth; 3.5 - 4.5 m;
Weight at birth: 500 - 800 kg;
Lactation: 1.5 - 3 years;
Mating season: late winter - early summer;
Birth season, northern hemisphere: January - August;
southern hemisphere: July - March;
Length of dives: 90 - 138 min.;
Depth of dives: 2,250 m (estimated 3,000);

Maximum speed: 30 km/hr
- **Distribution:** Broad distribution in all seas, with a preference for deep waters. There are geographical variations within the same species. The first subgroup recognized lives in the southern hemisphere and is known as *P. australianus*. In 1758, Linnaeus first described four species of the genus *Physeter* - *P. catodon*, *P. macrocephalus*, *P. microps*, and *P. tursio*. In 1823, G. Cuvier described sperm whales,

---

PLATANISTA GANGETICA
Roxburgh, 1801

- **Common names: En**: Ganges river dolphin; **Fr**: plataniste du Gange; **Sp**: platanista del Ganges; **It**: platanista del Gange
- **Significance of scientific name**
Platanista = assigned by Pliny the Elder, *gangetica* = from the Ganges River
- **Some data**
Maximum length: 2.6 m;
Maximum adult weight: 100 kg;
Life span: 28 years;
Age reaches sexual maturity: 10 years;
Gestation period: 8 - 9 months;
Length at birth: 0.90 m;
Weight at birth: 7.3 kg;
Lactation: 12 months

- **Distribution:** It lives in Nepal, in the Ganges delta, in the Brahmaputra River, the Meghna River and the Karnaphuli River in Bangladesh. This dolphin's population has been fragmented by the construction of dams along the entire river systems of the Ganges and the Brahmaputra, and this has also influenced its seasonal distribution, related to dry periods in the riverways in which it lives. This species' survival is threatened by pollution and exploitation of fish resources.

PLATANISTA MINOR
Owen, 1853

- **Common names: En**: Indus river dolphin; **Fr**: plataniste de l'Indus; **Sp**: platanista del Indus; **It**: platanista dell'Indo
- **Significance of scientific name**
Platanista = assigned by Pliny the Elder, *minor* = small
- **Some data**
Maximum length: 2.6 m;
Maximum adult weight: 85 kg;
Gestation period: 10 - 11 months;
Length at birth: 0.89 m;
Weight at birth: 7.3 kg;
Lactation: 12 months
- **Distribution:** Lives in the Indus River. Like its fellow species, the Indus River

■ *The two species, even if living in different areas, have the same shape, livery and morphology.*

dolphin is threatened by the construction of dams, which fragment the population and isolate groups, which are sometimes too small to ensure not only mating, but also an adequate genetic exchange.

Back sight

but did not give them any scientific name. Only later, based on a study by another naturalist, F. Cuvier, in 1836, did all cetologists adopt the name *P. macrocephalus* for all the varieties known. Today, a rereading of Linnaeus' work has led to acceptance of the present-day name. Whaling of sperm whales was banned in 1982, with the exception of kills from land bases in Japan, where whaling continued until 1988.

• **Curious facts:** The sperm whale reaches the greatest depths of any mammal. The deepest verified dive was by a sperm whale off the coast of Dominica in the Caribbean in 1991. Scientists from the Woods Hole Oceanographic Institute registered a dive 2,250 m deep within the span of an hour and 13 minutes. It is probable, however, due to the presence of deep sea animals found in gastric contents, that sperm whales can reach depths of 3,000 m.

PONTOPORIA BLAINVILLEI
Gervais and d'Orbigny, 1844

• **Common names: En**: franciscana; **Fr**: dauphin de La Plata; **Sp**: franciscana; **It**: pontoporia
• **Significance of scientific name**
Pontoporia = from the Greek *pontos* = open sea, *poros* = passage, *blainvillei* = from H. de Blainville, a famous French naturalist
• **Some data**
Maximum length: females 1.77 m, males 1.63 m;
Maximum adult weight: females 53 kg, males 43 kg;

Life span: 18 - 20 years;
Age reaches sexual maturity: 2 - 4 years;
Gestation period: 10 - 11 months;
Length at birth: 0.75 - 0.8 m;
Weight at birth: 7 - 8 kg;
Lactation: 9 months;
Depth of dives: 30 m
• **Distribution:** It was erroneously believed that this species moved from freshwater to the sea and vice versa; now it is known with certainty that it lives in the eastern coastal wasters of South

America, from the Valdez Peninsula in Argentina to the mouth of the Doce River in Brazil. The species is hunted, and its fat was once sold to make oil used to tan hides, as a lubricant and for waterproofing. Gervais and d'Orbigny first described this species as *Delphinus blainvillei* and later as *Stenodelphis blainvillei*.
Some authors place the franciscana and the baiji in the Pontoporiidae family.

PSEUDORCA CRASSIDENS
Owern, 1846

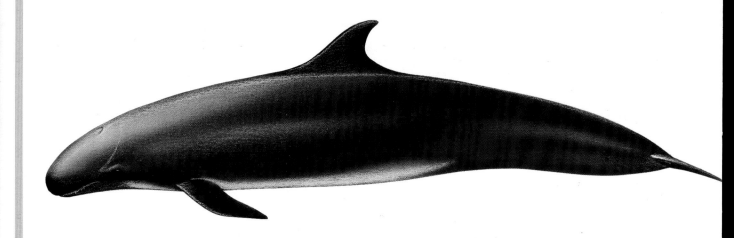

- **Common names: En**: false killer whale; **Fr**: faux-orque; **Sp**: orca falsa; **It**: pseudorca
- **Significance of scientific name**
Pseudorca = similar to killer whale; *crassidens* = with a large tooth
- **Some data**
Maximum length: females 5 m, males 6 m;
Maximum adult weight: females 1,2 t, males 2 t;
Life span: 20 years;
Age reaches sexual maturity: 8 - 14 years;

Gestation period: 11 - 12 months;
Length at birth: 1.8 m;
Lactation: 18 months;
Mating season: all year round
- **Distribution**: They live in all oceans of the world, in tropical, subtropical and warm temperate waters. They prefer the open sea, but can also be seen in partially closed seas. In 1846 Owen described this species from subfossil remains found in England and called it *Phocoena crassidens*,

believing it to be extinct. Following a massive stranding a few years later, it was realized that the species was still in existence. In 1862, Reinhardt published a description of these specimens, and due to its similarity to the killer whale, called it *Pseudorca crassidens*.
It is commonly hunted in Japan. The false killer whale interacts with the pelagic tuna hunt that takes place in the tropical Pacific, often becoming a victim of the nets.

SOTALIA FLUVIATILIS
Gervais, 1853

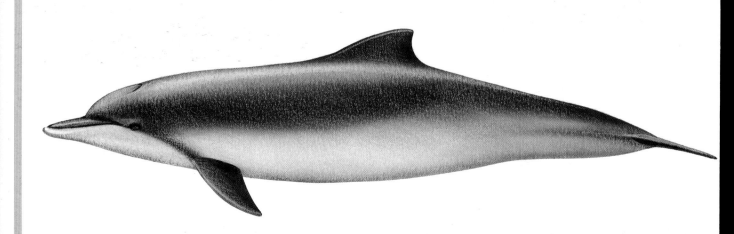

- **Common names: En**: tucuxi; **Fr**: sotalia; **Sp**: bufeo negro; **It**: sotalia
- **Significance of scientific name**
Sotalia = unknown, *fluviatilis* = river species
- **Some data**
Maximum length: in rivers - 1.52 m; in the sea - 2.6 m;
Maximum adult weight: 40 kg;
Gestation period: 10 months;

Length at birth: 0.7 - 0.8 m;
Mating season: January - February;
Length of dives: 80 sec.
- **Distribution**: Species limited to northeastern South America. Prefers murky, shallow waters. River populations swim up the Orinoco and the Amazon River system. It is currently believed that the genus *Sotalia* includes a single species

with two populations, one marine and the other freshwater, rather than the five species previously described (*S. brasiliensis*, *S. fluviatilis*, *S. guianensis*, *S. pallida* and *S. tucuxi*). This species has also been attributed to the Stenidae family, but it seems more accurate to place it in the Delphinidae family.

SOUSA CHINENSIS
Osbeck, 1765

SOUSA TEUSZII
Kukenthal, 1892

• **Common names: En**: Indo-Pacific hump-backed dolphin; **Fr**: dauphin à bosse de l'Indo-Pacifique; **Sp**: delfin jorobado del Pacifico negro; **It**: susa indo-pacifica
• **Significance of scientific name**
Sousa, of unknown origin, *chinensis* = from China
• **Some data**
Maximum length: females 2.5 m, males 3.2 m;
Maximum adult weight: 284 kg;
Length at birth: 1 m

• **Common names: En**: Atlantic hump-beaked dolphin; **Fr**: dauphin à bosse de l'Atlantique; **Sp**: delfin jorobado del Atlantico; **It**: susa atlantica
• **Significance of scientific name**
Sousa, of unknown origin, *teuszii* = from Edward Teusz, who collected the first specimen

• **Some data**
Maximum length: 2.8 m;
Maximum adult weight: 284 kg;
Length at birth: 1 m
• **Distribution:** Coastal species in West Africa. It is common in its area of distribution.

• **Distribution:** Coastal species. Fragmentary estimates indicate that this species is relatively common along the coast of Natal (in the Republic of South Africa) and in the mouth of the Indus River.

■ *The two species, even if living in different areas, have the same shape, livery and morphology.*

STENELLA ATTENUATA
Gray, 1846

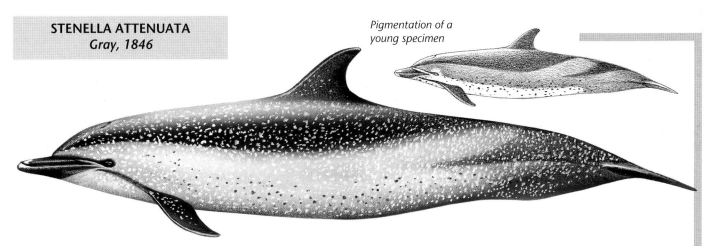

Pigmentation of a young specimen

• **Common names: En**: pantropical spotted dolphin; **Fr**: dauphin tacheté de pantropical; **Sp**: estenela moteada; **It**: stenella maculata pantropicale
• **Significance of scientific name**
Stenella = from the Greek *stenos* = narrow, *attenuata* = a little
• **Some data**
Maximum length in Pacific coastal area: females 2.07 m, males 2.23 m;
in Pacific oceanic area: females 1.87 m, males 2 m;

Maximum adult weight: 119 kg;
Life span: 45 years;
Age reaches sexual maturity: females 9 - 11 years, males 12 - 15 years;
Gestation period: 12 months;
Length at birth: 85 cm;
Birth interval for same mother: 2 or 3 years;
Lactation: 12 - 24 months;
Birth season: spring and autumn;
Maximum speed: 40 km/hr
• **Distribution:** Oceanic species, it has been sighted primarily in the eastern Pacific from

25°N to 15°S, where it is associated with schools of yellowfin tuna *(Thunnus albacares)*. In the Indian Ocean it has been sighted at 35°S.
Gray first called this species *Delphinus attenuatus*, then *Steno attenuatus*. Other synonyms are: *Delphinus brevimanus* (Wagner), *D. microbrachium* (Gray), *D. albirostratus* (Peale), *Steno capensis* (Gray), *Clymene punctata* (Gray), *Steno consimilis* (Gray) and *Prodelphinus graffmani* (Lönnberg).

STENELLA CLYMENE
Gray, 1850

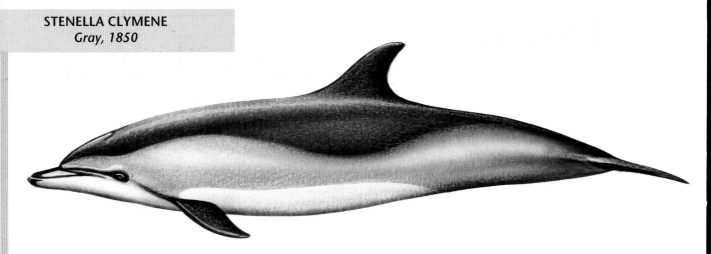

- **Common names: En**: clymene dolphin; **Fr**: dauphin de Clyméné; **Sp**: delfin clymene; **It**: stenella climene
- **Significance of scientific name**
Stenella = from the Greek *stenos* = narrow, *clymene* = the daughter of Oceanus and Tethys
- **Some data**
Maximum length: 2 m;

Maximum adult weight: 85 kg;
Length at birth: 1.2 m
- **Distribution:** Lives in the tropical and subtropical waters of the Atlantic Ocean. A pelagic species, it is believed to be fairly common, but nothing is known of the size of the population. This species' systematics was uncertain for a long time, due to morphological and anatomical

similarities with *Stenella coeruleoalba*, *S. longirostris*, *Delphinus delphis* and *Lagenodelphis hosei*. In 1981, Perrin and other collaborators confirmed the validity of this species.
From documented strandings, males and females appear to form separate schools and are often associated with the spinner dolphin.

STENELLA COERULEOALBA
Meyen, 1833

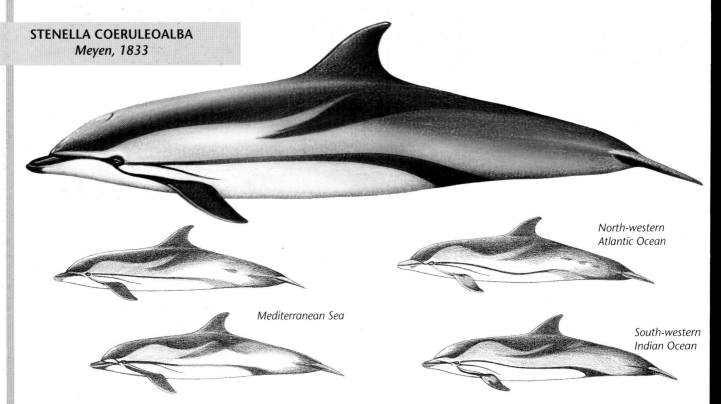

North-western Atlantic Ocean

Mediterranean Sea

South-western Indian Ocean

- **Common names: En**: striped dolphin; **Fr**: dauphin bleu et blanc; **Sp**: estenella listada; **It**: stenella striata
- **Significance of scientific name**
Stenella = from the Greek *stenos* = narrow, *coeruleoalba* = from the Latin, blue and white
- **Some data**
Maximum length: 2.56 m;
Maximum adult weight: 156 kg;
Life span: 57 years;
Age reaches sexual maturity: 9 years;
Weight at birth: 11.3 kg;
Gestation period; 12 months;

Lactation: 18 months;
Length at birth: 1 m;
Mating season: summer and winter
- **Distribution:** Prefers the tropical and subtropical waters of all oceans. In the Indian Ocean, it seems limited to north of 35°S, while in the eastern Pacific it is present between 35°N and 15°S. There are three stocks of striped dolphin in Japanese waters, one coastal and two pelagic.
Delphinus coeruleoalbus is the name Meyen gave this species in 1833. Its synonyms are *D. stix* (Gray, 1846); *D. euphrosyne* (Gray, 1846); *D. holboellii* (Eschricht, 1847);

D. lateralis (Peale, 1848); *D. tethyos* (Gervais, 1853); *D. marginatus* (Pucheran, 1856); *D. mediterraneus* (Loche,1860); *D. aesthenops* (Cope, 1865); *D. crotaphiscus* (Cope, 1865); *Tursio dorcides* (Gray, 1866); *Clymene dorides* (Gray, 1866); *Clymenia euphrosynoides* (Gray, 1868); *Clymene similis* (Gray, 1868); *Clymenia burmeister* (Malm, 1871); *Prodelphinus petersii* (Lutken, 1889), *D. amphitriteus* (Philippi, 1893) and *Stenella euphrosyne* (Oliver, 1922). Based on indications by the Scientific Commission, the International Whaling Commission has decided to revise this species' systematics by 1998.

STENELLA FRONTALIS
G. Cuvier, 1829

Pigmentation of a young specimen

• **Common names: En**: Atlantic spotted dolphin; **Fr**: dauphin tacheté de l'Atlantique; **Sp**: delfin pintado; **It**: stenella maculata atlantica
• **Significance of scientific name**
Stenella = from the Greek *stenos* = narrow, *frontalis* = frontal, of the front
• **Some data**
Maximum length: 2.29 m;
Maximum adult weight: 143 kg;
Length at birth: 0.88 - 1.2 m;

• **Distribution**: Lives only in the Atlantic Ocean, north to 48°N and south to 24°S. Prefers coastal areas. It is probably the most common dolphin in the Gulf of Mexico and the southeastern coast of the United States. In 1829, Cuvier described this species as *Delphinus frontalis*. The variability in colour and size depending on zone of distribution has caused confusion and errors in identification. The form found off the

northeastern coast of America used to be called *S. plagiodon* (Cope, 1866). Other synonyms are: *Delphinus froenatus*, *D. doris* and *D. plagiodon*. Fisherman from the Lesser Antilles, St. Vincent, St. Lucia and Dominica hunt it with harpoons. It is accidentally caught in stand nets along the western coast of Africa, Brazil and Venezuela.
Here it is also eaten or used as bait for shark hunting.

STENELLA LONGIROSTRIS
Gray, 1828

Typical pigmentation

• **Common names: En**: spinner dolphin; **Fr**: dauphin longirostre; **Sp**: estenela giradora; **It**: stenella dal lungo rostro
• **Significance of scientific name**
Stenella = from the Greek *stenos* = narrow, *longirostris* = with long rostrum
• **Some data**
Maximum length: 2.7 m;
Maximum adult weight: 77 kg;
Life span: 20 years;
Age reaches sexual maturity: females 4 - 7 years, males 6-9 years;

Gestation period: 10 - 11 months;
Lactation: 11 months;
Length at birth: 0.80 m;
Maximum speed: 20 km/hr
• **Distribution**: Prefers tropical and subtropical waters in all oceans.
In the eastern Pacific, its distribution is the same as the spotted dolphin. Hawaiian spinner dolphins are a separate population.
There appears to be a dwarf form in the Gulf of Thailand.

Gray described this species as *Delphinus longirostris* (1828), *D. alope* (1846), *D. microps* (1846) and *D. stenorhynchus* (1866). *D. roseiventris* (Wagner, 1846) should also be considered a synonym. According to Perrin and Gilpatrick Jr. (1994), there are three subspecies, *S. l. longirostris*, which is broadly distributed, *S. l. orientalis*, in the tropical East Pacific and the coast of Mexico, and *S. l. centroamericana*, on the western coast of Central America.

STENO BREDANENSIS
G. Cuvier, 1828

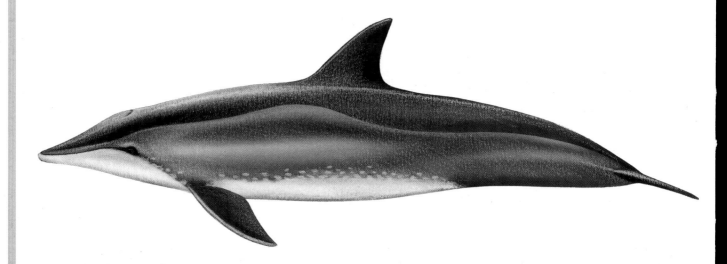

- **Common names: En**: rough-toothed dolphin; **Fr**: sténo; **Sp**: esteno; **It**: steno
- **Significance of scientific name**
Steno = from the Greek *stenos* = thin, referring to the rostrum, *bredanensis* = from Van Breda, an artist who first noted the species among Cuvier's material
- **Some data**
Maximum length: 2.8 m;
Maximum adult weight: 155 kg;
Life span: 30 years;

Age reaches sexual maturity:
females 10 years, males 14 years;
Length at birth: 0.80 m;
Depth of dives: 70 m
- **Distribution:** There is little information about this species. Sightings seem to indicate a distribution in tropical and subtropical waters. They live in deep water beyond the continental shelf, where surface water temperature is 25°C.
In 1960, Fraser and Purves placed the

genera Steno, Sousa and Sotalia in the Stenidae family, but nevertheless, accepted classification places them in the Delphinidae family.
It was originally described as *Delphinus rostratus* (Desmarest, 1817) and then as *D. bredanensis*. Other synonyms are *Delphinus planiceps, D. reinwardtii, D. chamissonis, D. compressus, D. oxyrhynchus* and *D. frontatus.*

TASMACETUS SHEPHERDI
Oliver, 1937

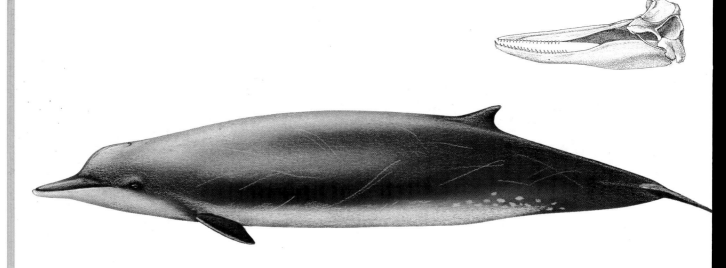

- **Common names: En**: Shepherd's beaked whale; **Fr**: tasmacète; **Sp**: ballena picuda de Shepherd; **It**: tasmaceto
- **Significance of scientific name**
Tasmacetus = the Tasman Sea; *shepherdi* = from G. Shepherd, curator of the New Zealand museum that described this species in 1933

- **Some data**
Maximum length: females 6.6 m, males 7 m;
Length at birth: 3 m
- **Distribution:** Rare species.
Its distribution is known only through strandings and a limited number of sightings near the coasts of New Zealand,

Australia, central Argentina, Tierra del Fuego, the Beagle Channel and Juan Fernandez Island in Chile. There are no synonyms or errors in identification. Oliver described this species in 1937 based on a complete skeleton conserved at the Wanganui Alexander Museum.

TURSIOPS TRUNCATUS
Montagu, 1821

Common name: **En**: bottlenose dolphin; **Fr**: grand dauphin; **Sp**: tursion; **It**: tursiope
• **Significance of scientific name**
Tursiops = marine animal similar to a dolphin, *truncatus* = with a short snout
• **Some data**
Maximum length: 4 m;
Maximum adult weight: 650 kg;
Life span: 30 years;
Age reaches sexual maturity: females 10 years, males 13 years;
Gestation period: 12 months;
Length at birth: 0.84 - 1.22 m;
Lactation: 12 - 18 months;

Mating season: summer on the European coast; spring and autumn on the Florida coast;
Depth of dives: 600 m;
Length of dives: 8 min.;
Maximum speed: 30 km/hr
• **Distribution**: Distribution from cold tropical waters to tropical waters in all seas. It is a primarily coastal species that lives in neritic waters. At present only one species is recognized. The subspecies (species according to some authors) described in the past are not universally recognized: *T. t. aduncus* (western Pacific and Indian Ocean),

T. t. ponticus (Black Sea), *T. t. gilli* (northeastern Pacific), *T. t. nuuanu* (tropical eastern Pacific), *T. t. gephyreus* (southwestern Atlantic) and *T. t. truncatus* (North Atlantic and other areas). Bottlenose dolphins are also hunted in the Philippines for food and as bait for the nautilus. This dolphin adapts most easily to captivity, and all dolphin aquariums in the world include this species.
Based upon indications by the Scientific Commission, the International Whaling Commission has decided to review the systematics of the genus *Tursiops* by 1999.

ZIPHIUS CAVIROSTRIS
Cuvier, 1823

• **Common names: En**: Cuvier's beaked whale; **Fr**: ziphius; **Sp**: zifio de Cuvier; **It**: zifio
• **Significance of scientific name**
Ziphius = from the Greek *xiphos* = sword, *cavirostris* = from the Latin *cavus* = hollow, and *rostrum* = rostrum or beak
• **Some data**
Maximum length: females 7 m, males 7.5 m;
Maximum adult weight: 3 t;

Life span: 36 years;
Length at birth: 2.7 m;
Length of dives: 40 min.;
Depth of dives: 1,000 m;
Maximum speed: 5 km/hr
• **Distribution**: Deep water species found in all seas with the exception of polar waters. The genus Ziphius is generally considered to have a single species, but

some authors believe a systematic revision is necessary based on the numerous morphological differences this species exhibits. There is little information on the size of this species' population, but the number of stranded individuals is the same as the total of all other species in the Ziphiidae family. Sightings are more frequent in underwater canyons or mountains.

168 A quartet of dolphins dances under the sea surface moving with incredible synchrony. The simpleness of the lines of their bodies has a harmony which exalts their movements that we can guess despite the static nature of the photograph.